The PR Knowledge Book

The PR Knowledge Book

Sangeeta Waldron

The PR Knowledge Book

Copyright © Business Expert Press, LLC, 2019.

Cover Image Credit: Jools Barrett, 195 Design House

First published in 2019 by
Business Expert Press, LLC
222 East 46th Street, New York, NY 10017
www.businessexpertpress.com

ISBN-13: 978-1-94999-164-2 (paperback)
ISBN-13: 978-1-94999-165-9 (e-book)

Business Expert Press Public Relations Collection

Collection ISSN: 2157-345X (print)
Collection ISSN: 2157-3476 (electronic)

Cover and interior design by Exeter Premedia Services Private Ltd., Chennai, India

First edition: 2019

10 9 8 7 6 5 4 3 2 1

Printed in the United States of America.

This book is dedicated to Steve and Rory Waldron, my husband and son; who are my dream team, who support me in everything I do. This book is for you—#teamwaldron—and of course my mum, who has empowered me, by giving me an education.

Praise for *The PR Knowledge Book*

"Knowledge is power and this book is powerful knowledge. Clear, direct and creative: it explains the digital landscape of PR for practitioners and clients alike."

> —**Julia Hobsbawm OBE**, editor-at-large, THRIVE Global, and author, *Fully Connected: Social Health in an Age of Overload*

"Smart and efficient PR is becoming even more critical now than ever for brands, with the advent of the digital world. *The PR Knowledge Book* from the expert Sangeeta Waldron helps businesses to unlock opportunities and to maneuver through challenges in a fast changing world. Highly Recommended."

> —**Jérôme Chouchan**, Godiva Chocolatier, president, Japan, South Korea, Asia, and Australia

"In a modern, digital, global business world, Sangeeta Waldron shows how to turn Public Relations into Personal Relations, which is absolutely essential to survive in the long run."

> —**Erik Korsvik Ostergaard**, leadership advisor, published author, and guest lecturer at the Copenhagen Business School

"Sangeeta is a seasoned PR professional and her wisdom is captured within this book. It's just what the doctor ordered!"

> —**Professor Jonathan A.J. Wilson**, PhD, partner at Dragonfly Black, LinkedIn Top Voices award winner

"This book provides extraordinary insights and provides real world lessons on how business leaders can employ PR to support their business objectives."

> —**Jill Totenberg**, CEO, The Totenberg Group, New York

"I greatly welcome this book that helps us reimagine PR as 'People Relations', a vital tool for empowering brand and business creation in a connected world."

—**Dr. Harbeen Arora**, founder, BIOAYURVEDA, ALL Ladies League, and Women Economic Forum, India

"Sangeeta Waldron has written a must-read for anyone wanting to do their own PR, wherever they may be in the world. Read this book—and learn from one of the best."

—**Rusen Kumar**, editor-in-chief, India CSR Network

"Sangeeta Waldron is a trusted colleague and inspiration. *The PR Knowledge Book* shares practical and proven strategies from the front lines of PR. She outlines the building blocks of creating a Brand and PR plan that delivers results by building relationships. Business is personal. It's about relationships. That's the bottom line."

—**Tami Belt**, author and founder, Blue Cube Marketing Solutions, Las Vegas

"Sangeeta Waldron has an intuitive understanding of what PR is and how it works. She is able to cut through the noise to simply and powerfully communicate an idea, and now, with her book, you can, too."

—**Tom Seabrook**, commissioning book editor, Jawbone Press

"As an entrepreneur this book is going to be permanently on my bookshelf. My go to guide on how to create publicity and deal with traditional and new media."

—**Raja Majid**, Las Vegas entrepreneur

"If PR has always baffled you, then this is the book to read. Written in an easy style with lots of examples. It will become your best-friend."

—*Asian Voice Newspaper*, the UK and Europe's leading Asian newspaper

"Sangeeta Waldron brings heart and soul to the business of PR. Her knowledge and wisdom were a key contribution to my organization finding its way through a rocky time. She is a superb educator in addition to being an outstanding practitioner of her art. A timely and valuable book."

—**Malcolm Stern**, Co-founder and Co-director

Abstract

The PR Knowledge Book is for everyone irrespective of where you are in the world—whether a student starting out in this industry or self-employed, a home business, small business, start-up, charity, or any other type of organization wanting to embark on your PR journey or just plain curious about what it entails. This book covers everything within the world of PR from how to create a brand, how to use social media, how to be newsworthy, to how to contact the media, how to have a global mind-set, the power of networking, and more. It is written in an easy style, packed with powerful tips, proven tools, and real-life case studies from around the world. In 12 chapters you will discover how to get your brand out there so you can attract clients and new business.

Keywords

brands; crisis; management; Facebook; global mind-set; Instagram; journalists; LinkedIn; measurement; media; networking; newsworthy; press releases; public relations; social media; storytelling; Twitter; YouTube

Contents

Foreword

S.E. Feinberg, author, screenwriter, and playwright

Andy Warhol once said, "Making money is art and working is art and good business is the best art." Warhol revolutionized the art world by recognizing and appreciating the power of public relations, and changed how we perceive commercial images—accepting those images as fine art—melding his art with what we already knew as familiar. When I hung a poster of a can of Campbell's soup on my wall, I was not only looking at a can of soup but was also remembering what the product meant to me, nostalgically—the necessity of the familiar.

The PR Knowledge Book brings public relations into the realm of necessity as we do business each day, because it reveals to the world what we hold dear—our products, ourselves, our dreams.

"It's all about the timing," Sangeeta often will explain to me, "everything has its time." Sangeeta is right. Timing is at the core of an effective public relations campaign—to control the dissemination of information at the right time, to the right people, in the right way. In Chapter 9, "Pitching to the Media," referring to disseminating stories to the news, Sangeeta points out, "Timing is Crucial—Find out the working hours of reporters and their deadlines so you can ensure your contact and supply of material caters to their needs." In Chapter 3, "The Press Release," we read, "Depending on the news story you will need to decide the timing of your story, so the journalists clearly understand when they can publish the story."

Case in point: Shortly after Sangeeta's friend and client, P.F. Sloan, the legendary composer, was given only weeks to live, she hopped on a plane to visit him—to take care of his professional needs at a time of imminent death, and to bid farewell to a dear friend. When she arrived in Los Angeles, I suggested that she wait until the next morning, because

Phil was feeling so poorly and could barely speak. He told me that he was embarrassed and would prefer to visit with her the next morning. Before Sangeeta arrived at the house, Phil passed. That day, Sangeeta and I got together. I was full of anxiety. Sangeeta was calm. "We must do this right," Sangeeta told me. "We must make sure that we control the copy that goes out to the press and control the who and the when."

Although so sad over the loss of our friend, we sat in a Starbucks on Melrose Avenue in Los Angeles and wrote the copy to announce to the world that the music of P.F. Sloan had come to an end—keeping the entire music world and fans of Phil unaware that they had lost him. In spite of this pressure, Sangeeta controlled the ball. She methodically moved through the process in the most pure form. This was PR at its best—grace under pressure, a balanced temperament, and the knowledge of what had to be done, with unflinching attention to detail.

"It's all about the timing," she pointed out. "What happens next?" I asked. "We give it to *Rolling Stone* first," she said. "They will expect it first."

After we wrote the copy, Sangeeta delivered the news to *Rolling Stone* and, in 15 minutes, every paper was picking it up. Radio stations were broadcasting it, the *New York Times, The Wall Street Journal,* and all the major newspapers and periodicals, hundreds and hundreds of stories around the world, as well as Internet and radio. Sangeeta's work, at a very critical time, insured that the legacy of her client was in place, and in order.

In my years of working with Sangeeta, I have learned to trust her as a person and depend on her instincts and wise counsel as a public relations professional. She is tenacious, sensitive, and brilliant. There is an efficient coolness to her method of communicating on behalf of her client. She possesses the precious gift of being able to explain the mechanics of her plan, simply and succinctly, as she lays out the art of public relations.

Sangeeta's methods are built on a bedrock of honesty, which in turn creates integrity, which in turn creates trust. In Chapter 2, "How to Be Newsworthy and What Is Fake News," she writes, "We need to be vigilant and on top of where our brand content is being placed. Media brands need to put reclaiming and maintaining consumer trust at the top of their agenda."

In Chapter 1, "The Basics of Public Relations," Sangeeta points out, "The fundamentals of PR are good communications, being able to tell your story in an easily understood way and for your story to have integrity and honesty." Further, she notes, "Every one of us is an individual whose character is made up of beliefs, values, and purposes that define who we are and who we connect with...."

I have been waiting for a book like this for a very long time. This will serve as an effective and required tool for those who desire to market themselves or their products to a competitive and complicated world. The mystery of public relations is unraveled in this essential work, *The PR Knowledge Book.*

Preface

I have always wanted to write a book since I was 12 years old and always had thought my first book would be fiction! Forty years later, I have written a business book focused on my trade and experience—public relations (PR)—and I could not be prouder. I have written this book in an easy style, demystifying the world of PR and media, making it a book for everyone irrespective where you may be in the world—whether you are a student starting out in this industry or a business, "homepreneur," mumpreneur, charity, start-up, or any other type of organization wanting to embark on your PR journey or just plain curious about what it entails.

When you work for yourself, you have to learn many different skills to survive. PR, social media, and marketing are probably the most important ones of all. Over the years, people have always asked me what is PR, and what does it actually do? What does it mean? Well, this book answers those questions, and shows you how to do it, particularly in today's digital and online world. Without getting your brand out there, how can you attract clients and new business? If you want to get ahead in the game, then this is the book for you. It has been written, and set out, to really help you get to grips with PR.

It is packed with powerful tips, proven tools, and real-life examples and case studies from around the world. By the end of this book you will realize that PR can change the trajectory of any business to become a winner.

CHAPTER 1

The Basics of Public Relations

We are all living in the era of digital communications, irrespective of where we might be residing globally. The United Nations in 2013 reported that more people in the world had mobile phones than access to a toilet. A staggering statistic and you may be wondering how does this fit into the context of public relations (PR) for a small- to medium-sized business or other type of organization? Well, it shows that over half of the world's population is now online, with the latest data showing that nearly a quarter of a billion new users came online for the first time in 2017. Africa has seen the fastest growth rates, with the number of Internet users across the continent increasing by more than 20 percent year-on-year (2018 Global Digital reports from We Are Social and Hootsuite).

Put this into the perspective of PR, it means digital communications is driving PR, where the three most important trends are affecting its future—social listening, digital storytelling, and real-time marketing. This in turn means there is no better time to be in business, an entrepreneur, an author, start-up, charity, or any other kind of small-sized to medium-sized organization. The power of success is with you and a strong PR plan.

This thought has been eloquently summed up by Mike Cherry, OBE, National Chairman, Federation of Small Business in January 2019, when he said,

> It has never been a more relevant time for a small businesses and the self-employed to put in place PR plans. Increasingly competitive markets, new export opportunities, diversification of audiences, fragmented and diverse channels of communications, as well as channels posed by regulations and cybercrime all create an environment of both opportunity and threat. PR is needed to

seize the former and minimize the latter. Many small businesses can also increasingly be effected by consumer generated content—from online reviews, to social media debate. This alone can make effective PR a must. (CIPR's A guide to selecting PR agencies and independent practitioners p. 3)

So, let me welcome you to the world of PR. An industry that involves creative ideas and thoughts, and then being able to communicate them via the media, which are magazines, newspapers, television, radio, and social media channels such as Instagram, Twitter, or YouTube.

PR is for everyone; there is no them or us—it is for all business types and sectors; everyone can benefit from this discipline. The purpose of PR is to raise the profile of an organization or promote a campaign/initiative—because we all know that age-old adage that "awareness drives consideration."

While everyone seems to know the term "public relations," not everyone really understands what it means. Many business and organizations understand that PR is a great way to build on their strategies and improve their online reputation, yet few really know what it involves. Essentially, it is about sending the right messages to the right places and people, to build your brand's reputation. It is a dynamic that could change the future of your business.

Why Is PR Important?

There are four reasons why public relations is important.

- *PR Increases Brand Awareness and Credibility*
  In any industry, trust plays a huge role in determining whether a business is successful; a lack of trust could mean that a brand loses opportunities. When you invest in PR, it can help to increase credibility by improving a business or organization's reputation through thought leadership pieces and media coverage, influencer connections, and networking strategies. The more people that are aware of your brand, the more success and opportunities you create for your business.

- *PR Enhances Your Online Presence and Profile*
  In a world where everyone is digitally connected, PR helps
  companies to make the most of their online presence through
  social media, press releases, and connections. With the right
  PR strategy approach, today's brands can make sure that they
  reach the right audiences.

- *PR Drives Profits, Sales, and Leads*
  Part of PR is marketing. When you enhance your reputation
  through a range of unique PR activities, you will be reaching
  out to new potential customers and clients, who will find
  more ways to connect with your business through your business stories, press releases, and online activities. PR will help
  you to craft the right messages to resonate with your target
  audience and then place your story with the right media; and
  now with online media, it means people can click and buy.

- *PR Changes the Way People Think About You, Your Brand,
  and Business*
  The trouble with the online world is that people can say anything they want about a company—regardless of whether it is
  true or not, and there is very little that business can do about
  it. Some businesses get a bad reputation unfairly, while other
  organizations are not on the right people's radar. By creating
  a PR plan to focus on PR campaigns, it can help turn these
  challenges around because the right actions and PR support
  can raise awareness for your brand in the right way.

The fundamentals of PR are good communications, being able to tell
your story in an easily understood way and for your story to have integrity
and honesty. To help us do this, I believe there are three wisdoms, which
we all need to imbibe before embarking on our PR journey and are:

1. Always remember that PR is about *people* and *relationships*;
2. *Business is always personal and about relationships*. We buy from
   people and brands we like;
3. *Trust your instincts*. Some of the best PR has been created by people
   trusting their instincts. Sir Richard Branson, the British entrepreneur who is fantastic at publicizing the Virgin brands, openly talks

about trusting his instincts and has said publicly, "I definitely go on gut instinct."

Knowing Your Brand

Before you get started on your PR plan and campaign, it is important to know who you are as a brand. Branding is just as important for small businesses as it is for big names. Yet the many small business owners I talk to, who understand that branding is essential to their business, still do not really know why. While others are confused about their own brand identity, if you do not know your brand, how can you expect others to know what you do and what you stand for?

Many small business owners recognize the link between successful businesses and strong branding and want to build a brand that creates similar success for themselves. They know that branding is not just a logo or how their business is perceived externally, but too few realize that successful brands have branding at the heart of their business. So much so that, you could almost substitute the word brand for business.

Branding is a way of defining your business to yourself, your team, and your customers/your external audiences. It could be called the business' "identity," but only on the understanding that it embodies the core of what the business is and its values, not just what it looks and sounds like.

Customers of all sorts of businesses are so savvy today that they can see through most attempts by companies to gloss, spin, or charm their way to sales. Therefore, the benefits that a *strategically defined brand* can bring are the same as when people fall in love with each other!

When customers connect—because they share the same values and beliefs as the brand—it leads to higher sales and better brand differentiation. A strong brand encourages loyalty and advocacy. It can even protect your price in times when competitors rely on promotional discounts to drive sales. Your brand can also give you the ideal platform from which to extend your offering or range. Here are ten tips on how to successfully create branding for your business:

1. *Start by defining your brand*
   Review the product or service your business offers. Pinpoint the space in the market it occupies and research the emotive drivers, rational

needs, and concerns of your customers. Your brand character should promote your business, connect with your customer base, and differentiate you in the market.

2. *When building your brand, think of it as a person*
Every one of us is an individual whose character is made up of beliefs, values, and purposes that define who we are and who we connect with—our personality determines how we behave in different situations, how we dress, and what we say. Of course, for people it is intuitive and it is rare that you even consider what your own character is, but when you're building a brand it is vital to have that understanding.

3. *What is driving your business*
What does it believe in, what is its purpose, and who are its brand heroes; these things can help establish your emotive brand positioning and inform the identity and character for brand communications.

4. *Aim to build long-term relationships with your customers*
Do not dress up your offering and raise expectations that result in broken promises, instead create trust with honest branding—be clear who your company is and be true to the values that drive it every day.

5. *Speak to your customers with a consistent tone of voice*
It will help reinforce the business' character and clarify its offering, so customers are aware exactly what to expect from the product or service.

6. *Do not try to mimic the look of big brands*
Try and carve out your own distinctive identity. There is now a big consumer trend toward independent businesses, and there have been several chains who have tried to mimic independents in order to capture some of the market. Truly independent operators can leverage their status to attract customers looking for something more original and authentic, which actually aligns with how they feel about themselves.

7. *Be innovative, bold, and daring—stand for something you believe in*
Big brands are bogged down by layers of bureaucracy, preventing them from being flexible and reacting to the ever-changing needs of their customers. Those layers of decision making can make it hard for them to be daring with their branding.

8. *Always consider your branding when communicating with customers*
Respect your customers' intelligence by not giving everything away up front. Generate some intrigue and allow them to find out more

about your brand for themselves. This is the way to foster both engagement and ambassadors who enjoy in telling other people what they have discovered.

9. *The future of branding is fluid and engaging*

Do not dilute your brand positioning with indiscriminate discounting. Promotions are an opportunity to reinforce your brand mission.

Defining your core brand values helps define your brand identity and guides all your company's decisions. Your organization's core values also make sure everyone is going in the same direction and automatically helps you to:

1. Attract better customers and staff;
2. Know how to pitch your business to the media;
3. What kind of collaborations and partnerships you are open to create and who you want to work with; and
4. If you are a service-led business, it helps you decide how and what you are selling.

Howard Schultz, who was the CEO of Starbucks from 1986 to 2000 and again from 2008 to 2017, as well as its executive chairman from 2017 to 2018, said, "If people believe they share values with a company, they will stay loyal to the brand" (SucceedFeed.com for Howard Schultz Quotes https://succeedfeed.com/howard-schultz-quotes/).

How to Define Your Brand Values?

I always recommend that a business should not have more than five brand values; five are easy to remember. Make them simple and that they are values that you believe in as an entrepreneur/business. People can see through anything that you are paying lip service to and they will need to be values that help define your services.

If you are able to get all the people in an organization rowing in the same direction, you could dominate any industry, in any market, against any competition, at any time. The good news is that core values can help you achieve this! The bad news is that in most organizations, if you ask four employees to articulate the company's core values, you get four different answers.

Some organizations have not set defined their core values, while other places created their core values years ago, where over time people and things have changed, as a result the core values need a refresh. Start by brainstorming a list and group similar ideas together, deleting those that are not essential. Some businesses base their values on sustainable initiatives and thoughts, while some are based on leadership and fairness.

Through discussion and reflection, you will eventually get to a short, key list. Make sure everyone in the business is genuinely happy with the core values. Once they are defined, announce them throughout the organization and use them; core values are meaningless if they are not used by everyone within the organization.

Case Stories

The iconic Coca Cola company defines its values on its official website under "mission and values" as:

- Leadership: The courage to shape a better future
- Collaboration: Leverage collective genius
- Integrity: Be real
- Accountability: If it is to be, it's up to me
- Passion: Committed in heart and mind
- Diversity: As inclusive as our brands
- Quality: What we do, we do well

A UK wellbeing client called Alternatives, a not-for-profit organization, which works with some of the biggest names in the wellbeing space, such as Deepak Chopra, Marianne Williamson, and Elizabeth Gilbert, created five key brand values:

- Love
- Integrity
- Compassion
- Inclusive
- Service

The Essar Foundation, which comes under the Essar Global Fund Ltd that is based in India, call their values the four P's:

- People
- Progress
- Power
- Passion

Another example is from a photographer, I worked with years ago, whose business is called Vivida Productions, who at that time, venturing into the world of videos specifically for the Asian wedding market, but he was not Asian himself and defined his brand values as:

- Films not videos—we produce beautifully, crafted films;
- Love and family are at the heart of what we do;
- We always work with integrity.

Today his brand value has evolved to, "bringing stories to life."

Once you have defined your brand values, do not shove them away in a drawer; be proud of them, display them where you and your staff can see them; and if you have a shop, where your customers can see them too. Remember they are powerful and important.

Strengths, Weaknesses, Opportunities, and Threats (SWOT)

After defining your brand values, I always think it is a good idea to create something called a *SWOT Analysis*, which stands for Strengths, Weaknesses, Opportunities, and Threats. It is an exercise used in marketing.

Years ago, when I started out as the first head of PR for a national UK organization called the National Federation of Women's Institutes, my mentor at that time introduced me to doing a SWOT Analysis and it was very useful, because it helped define the PR strategy I was attempting to write at the time. It is a tool that I still use today, even when I am trying to make home decisions. Again, there is nothing complicated about doing a SWOT Analysis, it is easy and just requires some quiet thinking. It works

Strengths	Weakness	Opportunities	Threats
Organic ingredients	No staff—just me	Social media and local media	Falling ill—no one to step-in
Everything is baked on the premises	Not enough time to do everything	Create a tasting event	Not able to bake enough produce
Some of the breads and cake recipes are family recipes—unique	New to area/community	Run a promotion on cakes	No staff resources
Trained baker	No one to do admin/stocks	Get in touch with local network groups	
Won an award on the course		Support a local charity	

Figure 1.1 SWOT analysis grid about here

whether you are an existing business or start-up. It helps to oversee a situation and can feed into your business strategy. It arranges your top strengths, weaknesses, opportunities, and threats into an organized list.

Your strengths and weaknesses are internal to your business—things that you have some control over, can change or improve. Examples include your expertise, knowledge, who is on your team, gaps in the team, reputation, and your location. Your opportunities and threats are external—things that are going on outside of your business. You can always take advantage of opportunities and protect against threats. Examples of these include competitors, new regulations, culture, technology, media, and customer shopping trends. You can always turn weaknesses into opportunities by finding solutions. Figure 1.1 presents a diagram of a SWOT Analysis, which has been completed by a start-up bakery run by one person.

The Power of the Story

The story is where we have all come from and has been part of our lives since the beginning of time. Stories connect us and are the best way to teach, persuade, and even understand ourselves. They are emotional, where we are more likely to remember and react to them. A compelling story, well told, grabs hearts and minds. The first printed story, the "Epic of Gilgamesh,"[2] was created and then begun to spread from Mesopotamia to other parts of Europe and Asia. The story was carved on stone pillars for all to see, which spread the tale around very quickly.

The advent of technology has and will continue to advance the power of the story. Technology is about sharing information; and sharing stories to create content is a key factor for personal branding and business success.

What Does Storytelling in Business Mean?

Storytelling is used as a tool in business in many areas, from leadership to branding to PR campaigns, messaging, and fundraising. We know that everyone loves a story, it helps to engage people to listen to you, and in PR, your story will help you in many different ways. From talking to the media, to being used on your "home or about page on your website" to being incorporated on your social media channels. Crucially, stories are the best way to distinguish yourself from the other brands in your industry.

We know that consumers are savvy and can smell if something is not "true" and, with social media and the Internet, you cannot get away with making things up. Not being truthful can end up creating negative publicity, which is a whole chapter—Chapter 10 to be exact!

You will hear a term, time and time again in brand storytelling, *engagement* and as with any content, the subject matter needs to be relevant and interesting if it is going to engage.

Therefore, the three important elements of a good story are:

1. Make sure it is your story;
2. Be authentic and real; and
3. Be engaging.

---

[2] The Epic of Gilgamesh is an epic poem from ancient Mesopotamia that is often regarded as the earliest surviving great work of literature. The literary history of Gilgamesh begins with five Sumerian poems about Bilgamesh, king of Uruk, dating from the Third Dynasty of Ur. For more into this story, go to Britannica's Epic of Gilgamesh (https://britannica.com/topic/Epic-of-Gilgamesh).

Major brands such as Lego and Coca Cola and have become industry icons because of their fondness for storytelling. If you rely only on your services and offering, you will become just another brand that is not able to differentiate itself from the others. You have to stand out.

Crafting Your Brand Story

Mark Truby, VP of Communications for Ford Motor Company, has beautifully summed up what makes a good brand story when he said, "A good story makes you feel something and is universal. They want to grasp your values and your commitment to excellence; be inspired and intrigued. Storytelling is the most powerful way to convey these ideas" (Marketing Week 2016).

Armed with your brand values and your SWOT Analysis to help you, you can now start to create your own brand story. Your brand story is about your passion of why you decided to start your business; it is why you do, what you do. It could be a childhood dream or love, or a hobby that has become an ambition. Start simple; use easy language, descriptive words. Write your past, present, and future story; incorporate your brand values. Your brand story is not about selling, it is about engaging and needs to resonate with your customers.

Case Stories

The Body Shop's brand story has stood the test of time and was the first in the beauty industry to make fair trade their priority; it completely revolutionized the whole sector. Founded by the late Anita Roddick who decided to open a small shop selling cosmetics. Anita traveled widely and wanted to use the rituals and customs she had encountered on her trips, into her back-to-nature products. Anita encouraged minimal packaging, including all forms of recycling and reusing, which was all about being sustainable. Anita also felt very strongly about animal testing. All these strong values helped shape the Body Shop's brand story from the very beginning. You can read more about the Body Shop and its founder, Anita Roddick by visiting their official website (www.bodyshop.com).

Nike is another famous brand story, which has been leveraging the power of great storytelling since 1999, when it released a one-minute commercial that commemorated the career of Michael Jordan. Nike was clever and ahead of its time; there was no mention of the brand itself in that film, until the end when the Nike slogan of "Just Do It" appeared at the end. Nike understood that this would make a lasting impression—it was an authentic story. ESPN on its website gives a wonderful insightful account into how Nike made this famous collaboration happen (http://espn.com/blog/playbook/dollars/post/_/id/2918/how-nike-landed-michael-jordan).

A wonderful and heartfelt brand story is from a small business working globally in children and adult learning difficulties, who started their business because of their own son who was diagnosed with autism. It was because of their own experiences of trying to find the right support, that they started their own organization.

This is another brand story, while again not a famous or a big brand, it still captures the spirit of a brand story. An online business passionate about the environment, called Unwrpd is an online store that wants to help consumers reduce their consumption of single-use plastics. Unwrpd has carefully tested and curated a selection of zero-waste alternative consumer goods, focusing on sourcing plastic-free, minimally packaged alternatives to disposable, single-use plastics and implementing buy-for-life and reusable products wherever possible.

I also love the brand story of Indian chef, Manoj Vasaikar originally from Mumbai, whose love and dedication to authentic Indian cooking with a twist has paid off, as he has founded his own restaurant, Indian Zing, which is a multi-award winning restaurant in London, hailed by leading food critics. His food is designed to follow the Indian principles of "Vastu Shastra,"[2] creating an environmental harmony between the five elements of earth, sky, fire, water, and air.

Know Your Stakeholders

All stories should be tailored to your stakeholders. Stakeholders take on many forms—internal employees, customers, governmental regulators,

---

[2] Vastu Shastra is an ancient Indian science of harmony and prosperous living by eliminating negative and enhancing positive energies around us. For more information go to Vastu Shastra Guru at https://vastushastraguru.com/

and even your competitors. A good story relates to the needs of those stake-holders; each may require a slightly different approach to creating the story.

Knowing Your Customers

Essentially this is knowing who you are selling to from a marketing PR per-spective who are your customers and who are you talking to. "Customer" can take on many different meanings. In a sales campaign, it may be who will purchase a product. In a governmental affairs campaign, it may be significant elected officials. In a corporate campaign, it may be internal employees. When you have defined who your customers are, you then know where you want to gain media coverage, what magazines you want to be featured in, what radio shows will have the right listeners for you.

Understanding your customer also means you know how to engage with them and what their interests will be, so you are able to create tai-lored products, services, and promotions—which are all in the PR mix.

Getting to know your customers is simple; you just have to talk to them, and you can do this through some simple market research.

There are a number of tools to help, some of which are free:

- If you have a website, Google Analytics is a great tool. It is free and generates detailed statistics about activity on a web-site. On its website, Google explains that the system "helps you analyze visitor traffic and paint a complete picture of your audience and their needs, wherever they are along the path to purchase" (Google; https://marketingplatform.google.com/about/analytics).
- Conduct an online survey, where you can create a question-naire and send it to your social media followers and/or e-mail subscribers and then quantify the results. To get people to participate in the survey, incentivize with a prize or reward.

Start to get to know your customers personally. This is one for more established businesses. Take some extra time to get to know them on a personal level—remember PR is about relationships. Find out what they are concerned about when they talk to you. What appeals to them, or excites them?

Knowing Your Competitors

What you do not want to do is copy or imitate your competitor, because how do you then attract customers? There is room for everyone and clients will buy from the business and brands that appeals to them, which could be based on your brand values, your brand story, and how well you know your customers. I believe the streets of New York City demonstrates this perfectly and, when I am there, I enjoy walking down the streets in the early mornings, where you will find different independent coffee houses, side-by-side, all buzzing and busy with customers. It shows how there is room for everyone and that customers will buy from the businesses that they like and "buy into."

I have worked with so many businesses and start-ups who want to be just like their competition including their website design, their logo look, and feel. I always say, "How will visitors know that they have landed on your website, if you look just like your competition?!"

Be bold, be different. It also allows you to take on new trends and be newsworthy, which is very attractive to the media, who are always looking for new ideas, new products, and new brands—because that makes news.

Summary

Chapter 1 gets us off to a good and firm start, where we now have a strong understanding of PR, where it has been demystified and broken down. You are now ready to define your brand, work on your brand story, identify your audience, and know who your competitors are; these are the main ingredients to getting started on your PR journey. With these in place, you will be ready to start thinking about how to be newsworthy, which is the focus of the next chapter.

In Chapter 2, we get to grips with how your news story will be the backbone of your PR campaign, which essentially is your pitch to the media and can determine the success of your PR activities. We will look at how to hone your media message, which further helps to build brand awareness, and yes, it all fits and loops together, back to what you have learnt here in Chapter 1.

CHAPTER 2

How to Be Newsworthy and Fake News

Your news story is the most important part of a strong PR campaign and is also known as your "pitch" to the media. It is essential to get this right, as your story will determine the success of your PR campaign.

There are quite a few things to think about and work out when you have a news story, but the first one would be to decide what makes news? As not everything is "newsworthy."

What Makes News Checklist

This following checklist will help you make that call:

1. *Timing*—You want to work ahead and plan your stories.
   If your own news story can ride on a current news topic, then you potentially have strong news story and these days we can see what is trending on Twitter, which clearly shows what is "news in real time." This also means that as consumers we are used to receiving constant updates, and because there is so much news about, old news is quickly discarded. Ensure your news is timely.
2. *Significance*—The number of people affected by the story is important. If it affects a community, a sector, a vast number of people that means more of us will be interested to read the story and as a result the media will be interested to run the story.
3. *Location*—Stories that happen near to us have more significance. The closer the story to home, the more newsworthy it is. However, location does not have to mean geographical distance, as stories from countries with which we have a particular bond or similarity have the same effect.

4. *Celebrities*—We are living in a celebrity-led culture and famous people get more coverage just because they are famous! If you have a local celebrity or a global star endorsing your product or attending your event, the media will be interested. It could even be a quote or message of support. This is why lots of charities try to get well-known names on board as supporters, because it helps make their cause more attractive to the press.

5. *Human Interest*—This one is a particularly good one for small businesses; a news story with a human interest angle is always attractive for the media, because as we know, we all love a story, as they appeal to our emotions. They evoke responses, such as happiness or sadness, and these kinds of stories are not time-sensitive because they do not date as quickly. Television chat shows, news programs, and radio like good strong human interest stories.

   However, before you put a human interest news story forward, and if using a case story, always ask the person's permission first—that is if they are happy for their personal story to be sent to the media. I have known small businesses who had great human interest stories sourced from their client base and decided to pitch these stories to their local news, without asking their clients if they were happy to speak to the press. Needless to say, this became messy.

6. *Launch of Products*—You might have a product that you are bringing to market that is newsworthy in itself because it is eco-friendly, innovative, and different than anything else. Make sure you have a few samples that you can send to the press.

7. *Surveys/Reports and Books*—If you have commissioned a report or have some strong data that is revealing new findings, then this could be newsworthy. Again, the report needs to be accurate and timely. Sometimes the media are interested in reports or data in advance of their official publication dates.

8. *High-Quality Images*—Always have good images to go with your story, which should also be of high quality, so they can be reproduced online and in the print media.[1] Clearly label your photo and

---

[1] The quality of images needs to be sharp and recommend that images have a resolution of a minimum of 300 dpi, while some media outlets might prefer a JPEG file over an Adobe Illustrator or Photoshop file.

identify those in the photos from left to right. Again, check that everyone in the picture is happy for the photo to be circulated to the press. It is also important to credit the photographer who has taken the photo, particularly if you have used a professional photographer.

9. *Events*—Annual events, conferences, and launches can be newsworthy, especially if you have interesting keynote speakers and high-profile guests. It is important that you contact the media well in advance, to ensure that they can get the event in their daily schedule diary. Offering free press passes to paid events is the norm and reserving their seats at the event is protocol.

10. *Fact Check*—Always make sure your facts are correct, spellings of people's names are accurate, and that any information in the news stories such as contact details are all on point. There is nothing worse than getting that story published, only to see glaring errors within the article.

Local or National Media?

I discuss this in more detail in Chapters 8 and 9, but the top line is, once you have worked out if your story is newsworthy, you then need to decide if the story is for local or the national media; and that is based on *impact*. Announcements that have local impact are newsworthy for local media outlets. If your story is going to impact people nationwide, then you will pitch your story to the national press. If your news story is related to your trade/sector and will be something your peers will want to know, then this is a good story for the trade press.

Here are some pointers:

- If you are a human resource (HR) consultant and you have written a book about leadership in the workplace, then contacting the HR media is the perfect fit for this story. Or if you are a Bitcoin organization then the financial press and financial journalists would be the media for you to contact.
- Depending on the impact of your story, you may want to consider contacting the news desks or news editors within the media as impact stories can be time-sensitive. Every media outlet, whether TV, radio, or national or local papers, has a news desk and an editor.

- Do not forget to contact online influencers, Instagrammers, and bloggers who may be interested in your story, especially if you are launching a product. They have a big reach and following that can be just as effective as the traditional media of TV, radio, and print.

- However, sometimes with the best will in the world and all the calls, the media may not be interested in your story—and that is just because they get so many news stories every day, every hour, every minute. This does not mean that you cannot do something with your story, and it is a lost opportunity, because you can use social media to get your story out. Apart from sharing the story on your social media channels such as LinkedIn, Facebook, Twitter, and Pinterest, you can also write your own news story as a blog post and upload on it on your website. You can share it online and amplify your own news story by using "hashtags" (e.g., #theprknowedgebook) and tagging those influencers who you think will be interested in your news story into your post. Influencers include audiences such as your peers, industry experts, clients, and relevant media.

Depending on how well your story does online, sometimes the mainstream media may pick up the story and decide to feature the story. You could also create your own video or podcast.

Fake News

I do not think I could write this chapter without including something about the phenomena of *fake news*, which mostly happens online. These are news or stories on the Internet that are not true. From Russian "bots" to charges of fake news, headlines are awash with stories about dubious information going viral. Fake news spreads much faster than real news; it is much easier for these stories to spread quickly, which can be a problem. Nowadays, it is easier than it used to be to edit photos and create fake websites and stories that look realistic.

What makes a news story fake? Well, that is tough one to answer, but essentially it is a story that cannot be verified. It either does not contain any links to its sources or, if there are links, they stay within the domain or send you to articles that are not relevant.

Fake news is a problem for different reasons, but mainly because it takes away from real, authentic news. It is also a problem because it can make people believe things that are completely untrue and is peddling lies. These stories tend to play on our emotions; they make us angry, happy, or scared.

When people publish something without checking that it is completely accurate, it can make people have less trust in the media, as well as make everyone believe something that might be untrue—and people only tend to share things that they agree with. So, if people are sharing a lot of fake news and lots of people believe it, it is easy to get sucked into a bubble that is actually completely different to the real world—and a long way from the truth.

Lazy journalism can also contribute to fake news and stories that may have some truth to them, but they are not completely accurate. This is because the people writing them do not check all of the facts before publishing the story, or they might exaggerate some of it.

Fake news is becoming more and an problem, particularly for brands, as fake news can affect reputations. It is important that we all become more discerning about what we are reading and sharing. It does not take too much imagination to see a scenario where your brand becomes the victim.

Equally, brands should take responsibility for what they can control. We need to be vigilant and on top of where our brand content is being placed. Media brands need to put reclaiming and maintaining consumer trust at the top of their agenda.

Summary

There are lots of things to consider as a business or organization when you want to make "news" and the checklist in this chapter is a useful aid, especially when it comes to who you should be contacting, that is whether it is national or local media. Just on that, do not forget how powerful and supportive your local press can be. So, with your news story defined, you will need to send your story out via something called a *press release*, which is unique to PR. In Chapter 3, we learn what is exactly a press release and importantly, how to write one, a good one!

CHAPTER 3

The Press Release

Now with your defined new story, the next step is to get your story out, which is communicated through something called a *press release*, which you as a business will need to create and draft. The press release is one of the main components of PR and there is a common phrase in PR, which is that your press release will need to be "attention grabbing."

Press releases are also referred to as a *news release* and is the medium that you send your story to the media. A good press release adds values to your brand and business, from helping to grow brand identity to strengthening your image as an industry thought leader, and allows for exclusivity.

We are going to look at the relevance of the press release and, importantly, find out how to write and format one using an example. I will also expand on the difference between a press statement/announcement, which is different from a release, and finally how to distribute your press release. The key thing to remember is not to be daunted. I often describe them as short, snappy letters to the media, without the "dear" salutations, and they become easier to write with practice.

Before we look at how to write and put a press release together, it is important that we put the press release into context into today's digital world. About 20 years ago the press release was the only way that PR professionals could send out their story to the media. However, things are changing, and social media has influenced this change and there is some evidence that the news release is in decline.

A report by two influential media organizations, who together surveyed more than 500 journalists revealed that that 53 percent in the United States and 41 percent outside the United States do not use press releases to find new story ideas (Muck Rack and Zeno Group 2018).

The survey also revealed that only three percent of journalists globally said that they relied heavily on them. This report also showed that sending press releases is not entirely a fruitless activity. While 21 percent of journalists based in the United States and 36 percent of journalists based outside the United States said they "somewhat" rely on press releases, 16 percent of journalists globally use press releases. Well-written and properly formatted press releases serve as brand identifiers for your business or organization. So, with this statistic in mind how do you draft one?

How to Write a Press Release—Format and Style

Like everything in life, writing a press release is easy, when you know how. The written style is simple sentences that give information to a journalist, blogger, or perhaps a trade event or event organizer about your news story. There are certain elements of a release:

- *Press Release Template*
  Most organizations create a simple template for their press releases that can be done as a word document. It means that the term "Press Release" or "Media Release" is clearly stated, so that the media understand it is a press release and know it holds a news story.
- *Logo and Branding*
  At the very top of the press release is the opportunity to include your logo and brand the press release.
- *Date/Timing*
  Depending on the news story you will need to decide the timing of your story, so the journalist/media influencer clearly understands when they can publish the story. There are two options; if your news story is not time-sensitive and the media can publish your story immediately, you will state near the date, "For Immediate Release."

  However, if your news story cannot be published immediately, then you will need to reference it and say, "Embargoed," stating what date and time it can be used. Embargoed press releases are usually used for reports and surveys that will be published in the future. Once a journalist sees an "embargoed release," if interested in the news story, they will contact you to agree and coordinate a date and time of when they would like to publish the story. Occasionally, if the news story is really strong and the media or journalist is very high profile, an embargo can be broken and the story can be

published in advance. This story is called an "exclusive" and only that particular high-profile media or journalist will run the story with your agreement that you will not allow another journalist or media outlet to publish the story in advance of the embargo.

This is how the media and high-profile journalists raise their own profiles by recognizing strong stories and running them exclusively.

- *Contact Details*

  At the top of the press release you also need to include the contact details of who the media can immediately contact for more information about the news story; and if you are a small business or organization, this could be someone in your team who fully understands the story, as you may not want to be inundated with all media requests for information. Once, the appropriate person has been identified, their name along with their direct e-mail and a direct phone number are added to the release. If a journalist is running against the clock, nothing frustrates them more if they cannot find the contact details or that the person dealing with the news story is not available.

- *Press Release Title*

  Every press release needs a strong, effective title. They do not need to be clever, but if possible to be engaging in order to attract the attention of the journalist or media influencer. Remember your press release is not the only release hitting the in-box of a journalist or news desk. Sometimes just stating what it is about is good enough.

- *The Press Release's First Paragraph*

  The first paragraph of a press release is key and there is a PR golden rule that it should include the "Five W's" of "who, what, where, when and why." Those five questions should be answered in the opening statement of a press release, so a busy journalist can read it quickly and find out everything that they need to in that one read.

- *The Body of the Release*

  The rest of the press release goes on to explain the fuller and more detailed story, using any quotes and data. If your press release runs to more than one typed page, indicate this on the release at the bottom saying in bold text "More Follows or "MF" and insert the press release on the subsequent page(s) with the page number in brackets so the journalist immediately knows what page they are reading and if anything is missing.

- *Notes to Editors*

  There is something called "notes to editors," which is at the very end of the press release and are short factual bullet points where the journalist can immediately know who to contact for more information with their contact details, what website to look at, and anything else relevant to the news story.

Figures 3.1 and 3.2 provide press releases that break over two pages, the purpose of the story announces the UK's national curry award.

What is a Press Statement?

There is a distinct difference between a press release and a press statement. We now know that a press release is issued in relation to a news story, while a press statement is released in reaction to an event or occurrence.

A press statement is short, contained, and to the point. It can be a brief explanation, a pithy quote, or a response to the news about you. A statement is instant and can be released much more quickly than a traditional press release. It also holds contact information for follow-up.

Press statements are usually made by governments or large corporates to protect their reputations, and may be drafted in consultation with their

Bangladesh Caterers Association Press Release

Immediate Release: 2 October 2017

For all media enquiries contact: X on Mobile: x; Email: x

Bangladesh Caterers Association Announces This Year's Search For Britain's Best 'Curry House' and 'Chef of the Year'

On 4 October, 2017 at the Palace of Westminster, Grimond Room in Portcullis House between 2pm to 4pm, Dr. Rupa Huq, MP will host the Bangladesh Caterers Association (BCA), who will announce this year's exciting search to find Britain's best 'Curry House' and 'Chef of the Year'. The winners will be announced at a special star-studded event on 19 November at the Park Plaza, Westminster Bridge, London.

These Awards are now in its 12th year and a key event for the UK's food and hospitality sector, which is much anticipated by all. BCA will recognise the achievements of outstanding restaurants and talented chefs, who all have the skills to create curries full of flavours and aromas, including presentation. The Awards reignites Britain's love affair with curry, which is very much a part of mainstream culture and the country's DNA.

In these politically uncertain times, it's communities and the love of good food that brings people together and BCA has been doing exactly this since 1960 - sourcing Britain's curries and continuously striving for innovation and perfection. The theme of this year's Awards is BCA: **Sourcing Britain's Love for Curry Since 1960.**

While these Awards are a time of celebration, there is also an underlined message that the BCA wants to get across. It's an organization representing 12,000 plus British Bangladeshi restaurants and takeaways in the UK, and like many small businesses across the country they are facing hard times. The two main issues that the BCA wants to highlight this year are:

More Follows

Figures 3.1 Example of press release

Bangladesh Caterers Association Press Release

Bangladesh Caterers Association Announces This Year's Search For Britain's Best
'Curry House' and 'Chef of the Year' (2)

1. The shortage of skilled chefs, which has led to closure of restaurants;

2. For Restaurants and Takeaways, the current flat rate VAT threshold is £150,000 where a caterer pays 12.5% if the yearly turnover is £150,000 or less. It would help a lot of caterers if this threshold was raised to £250,000; as VAT rate of 20% is considered to be very high and unaffordable; for most caterers their annual turnover is between £150,000 and £250,000. The BCA has taken a resolution to lobby government to raise the threshold to £250,000.

ENDS

Notes to editors:

*   For all media enquiries, press tickets to the BCA Awards please contact x; Mobile:x; Email:x

*   BCA Award visit www.bca1960.com

*   This year's theme for the awards is - BCA: **Sourcing Britain's Love for Curry Since 1960** and hashtags are #curry #BCAAwards Find us on Twitter @BCA1960

Figures 3.1 (Continued)

For all media enquiries and any image requests please contact: Sangeeta Waldron;
M: +44 (0) 7786542776; E: sangeeta@serendipitypr.co.uk

Date: Immediate Release

LID Publishing Signs Antonio Nieto-Rodriguez - One of the World's Most Influential
Thinkers in Management and Leadership as its Author (1)

LID Publishing, the fifth largest publishing house in Europe for business books, who is celebrating its 25th Anniversary this year is thrilled to announce that it will be publishing the world renowned champion of project management and strategy implementation, Antonio Nieto-Rodriguez's second book, *The Project Revolution*.
Nieto-Rodriguez is a Thinkers50's award winner and LID Publishing's global business journal, *Dialogue*, produced in association with Duke Corporate Education, part of Duke University is a media partner to Thinkers50. *Dialogue* will be supporting Thinkers50 Europe this September.
Nieto-Rodriguez is a *Dialogue* writer and Duke CE educator, and LID Publishing through *Dialogue* has been a supporting his work and ideas for some time. This 'circular relationship' truly reflects LID Publishing's avant-garde approach to publishing, adopting a project based model, that allows it to stay ahead of the curve compared to other publishers.

LID fought off publishing giants to win this book deal with Nieto-Rodriguez, who wanted an innovative project based publishing agency. Nieto-Rodriguez believes **projects have the flexibility and the agility to react and adapt; and predicts that projects are becoming the essential part of the organisation of the future.**
Antonio Nieto-Rodriguez says: "From my first contact with LID Publishing, I noticed that LID treated authors differently - like they knew me personally. I discovered a reputable brand with a clear purpose and a great team behind. LID Publishing offered me a fair deal and an innovative approach to publishing. Despite having other options, LID was precisely what I was looking for; a long term partnership to share and communicate my views across the world."

Niki Mullin, Business Development Director, LID Publishing says: "We are delighted and proud to be publishing Antonio Nieto-Rodriguez's next book. This is big news in the business book publishing world, as LID Publishing beat well-known names in the publishing world to sign him. It is a testament to LID and what we do; because we do it well. We publish great and inspiring books that fuel the minds of readers. If there are any authors out there reading this, I encourage them to get in-touch."

ENDS

Notes to editors:

For all publishing enquiries please contact Niki Mullins Business Development Director on M: +44 (0)7764 989 599; E: niki.mullin@lidpublishing.com

For information about LID Publishing please visit: www.lidpublishing.com and/or @LidPublishing on Twitter.

To mark its 25th Anniversary, LID Publishing is *one of the new signatories for the National Literacy Trust's '2018 Vision for Literacy Business Pledge.'*

Antonio Nieto-Rodriguez's first book was *The Focused Organisation* published by Routledge in 2012.

Figure 3.2 Example of longer press release with editor notes

legal teams. These days' press statements are also issued on social media, particularly by celebrities to protect their brands.

If you are ever in the position of making a statement, do select your words carefully and, if unsure about something, consult with your legal counsel before you make a public announcement.

Here is an example of a press statement made by Ja Rule in connection with the now infamous Fyre music festival on Twitter. He was associated with the festival, which was a product of Fyre Media, a booking company from rapper Ja Rule and his tech partner Billy McFarland (@Ruleyork 2017):

> We are working right now on getting every one of the island SAFE that is my immediate concern…[sic] I will make a statement soon I'm heartbroken at this moment my partners and I wanted this to be an amazing event it was NOT A SCAM as everyone is reporting I don't know how everything went so left but I am working to make it right by making sure everyone is refunded…I truly apologize as this is NOT MY FAULT…but I'm taking responsibility I'm deeply sorry to everyone who was inconvenienced by this…

Press Release Distribution

So, you are now ready to send out your news story and there are ways to do this; if your press release is for your local or trade media, you can easily search for your local or trade press online and e-mail out your press release.

Make sure you share it via your social media channels, so tweet it out, out it on your Facebook page, and of course your business website.

If your press release is national or global, then if you have the budget you could think about investing in buying the services of press release distribution outlet. A press release distribution service will have a complete database of all the media relevant to your news story in your region, country, and globally. There are many such services and can be found online and it is worth shopping around.

Depending on the number of press releases you are sending out a month or year, you can have subscription services and is one to think about.

Summary

Everything you do in PR has a purpose, and the press release is an important vehicle to communicate your business news message to the media. They have a hidden power, where the key to drafting press releases well, is to focus them on newsworthy events. They are great for sharing timely, relevant news such as an event or a product launch. Press releases are practical and informative; there is no need for creative writing skills. Instead, it is about providing the facts about your business story in a clear and easy-to-read format; where the more you do them, the easier they become to write. While they may sound old-fashioned, they still have a place in today's high-tech news world. They go alongside the rise of social media stars and celebrity endorsements, which is the focus of Chapter 4, "Social Media Influencers and Celebrity Endorsements." Whether we admit it to ourselves or not, we can all become a little starstruck and, in business, high-profile personalities can add value to our brands, our news stories, events, and campaigns.

CHAPTER 4

Social Media Influencers and Celebrity Endorsements

Social media influencers, Instagrammers, bloggers, and vloggers can positively impact a PR campaign along with celebrities, who are our famous film, music, sport stars, authors, and TV personalities. While it may seem very glamorous of working with celebrities, like everything there are pros and cons of working with them. These relationships, irrespective of who you are working with, will need a level of commitment from your side to invest and nurture these relationships.

Social Media Influencers

Social media influencers have boosted the PR media tool box when it comes to reaching today's audience. The digital world has shifted the balance of power between consumers and brands, where now consumers are more likely to trust the people they see on their social media feeds than traditional PR marketing methods. We have become a society, irrespective of where we are in the world, of "scrollers," where we are constantly going through our phones searching for information, ideas and things, and when we see something that we like, we click, and we buy it.

So, by incorporating the rise of these social media influencers into your public relations strategy, your business will be able to reach larger audiences, promote positive branding, and increase customer engagement and awareness.

Micro-Influencers

One of the ways to approach working with these social media stars, especially if you are a small local business or charity, is to work with smaller or otherwise known as micro-influencers who will have a close-knit community of less than 10,000 followers, instead of larger, national influencers (mega-influencers) who are more difficult to engage and get hold of. While being less known than their more prominent counterparts, micro-influencers have become a driving force behind the influencer marketing industry's growth and development. They make up the largest portion of influencers and are across multiple niches and platforms.

Social media is part of their daily routines, which means they understand the importance of *authenticity* and of nurturing their online communities with valuable content in an accessible way. These characteristics means that their engagement is far stronger than the mega-influencer. Their smaller followings will actually be a far better fit to target the stakeholders you want to engage, as they will have higher engagement rates than influencers who boast millions of followers; engagement is key when looking at social media success. We see a lot of this kind of activity on Instagram, where Instagram stories are big and have power.

You could also think about collaborating with micro-influencers who are based locally to you; as again, being from the local area means they can influence high engagement locally, which will allow your business and the influencer to connect with actual people in your target market/ community.

There is often a cost to engaging a social media influencer as you are paying for their time, engagement, commitment to your brand, and influence. Do look at your own social media following and see if you already have someone who fits the bill. An influencer who is already engaging with your brand can be easy to engage.

Where Do You Find Social Media Influencers?

YouTube® is home to lots of social media influencers and before the advent of Instagram this was where many of them found their rise to fame. Research shows that YouTube®'s audience are young because there is a little bit more depth to the story and they are more like TV shows.

The United States and the United Kingdom are certainly ahead when it comes to understanding the worth of Instagram influencers. That said, other countries are catching on and I am pretty sure that the trend of using Instagram influencers to market products and services will take other regions by storm too and this can be seen in countries like India and Brazil.

Case Stories

A new fresh online fashion brand for women that is based between Taiwan and the United Kingdom wanted to break into the UK market. The fashion market is notoriously difficult to enter, and our budget was small. We wanted to grow the brand's social media following quickly, so we decided to work with two different types of social media influencers who would love the brand. We identified the two we thought had synergy and approached them both. One of the two was a micro-influencer with about 12,000 followers. During the collaboration she was quick to respond, easy, and friendly to work with, and posted photos and videos of herself in some of the outfits that she had selected herself from the fashion brand's collection, giving her own thoughts why she liked the pieces she had chosen. This micro-influencer was not paid but kept the pieces that she promoted. Her followers trusted her endorsement of the brand, drove brand awareness, and boosted online sales. We were also able to share the posts and photos on Twitter and Instagram.

Another one of my clients was an American singer-songwriter, who had been well-known in the 1960s. He had just written his memoirs, but needed to be relevant to the current music industry and appeal to a new generation of listeners who had probably never had heard of him, even though his past work had influenced a lot of what they were listening to now. Luckily, timing wise, there was a current, young, and popular female artist who had recently covered one of his songs. She has a strong online influence and her followers would also be interested in this American musician. There was a connection and a commonality. I approached her to see if she would be interested to connect with my client and write the foreword to his book; she was happy to do so. This approach became a long-lasting relationship, where this female artist gave her full support and commitment to this artist. They did a lot of music events together, gained a lot of media coverage, and had success together.

Being in PR you get to work with lots of photographers and I met a new photographer starting out who was new to the photography world.

Figure 4.1 Relationship of brand to social media influencer

She hailed from an advertising background, where she has successfully turned her passion and hobby into a business. She started to specialize in family portraits, yet at the same time she also wanted to work with some of the "mumpreneurs" who were storming it on Instagram as social media influencers. So, she started to go to the events where they would be, being the official photographer at these events. People got to know her and now she takes their pictures—and gets paid well, credited and is in demand.

Figure 4.1 presents a simplified formula to increase the impact and outcome often associated with the use of social media influencers in public relations.

Working with Celebrities

Working with celebrities is a little similar to working with social media influencers, though invariably you will not have direct access to them; you will have most of your conversations via their agents and managers. These high-profile personalities have a big team supporting them from their own publicists, and as mentioned agents and managers. Not all these various teams are under one roof and will be working at different companies, so the communication process can be frustrating and at times challenging. A lot of work and commitment goes into maintaining and supporting these relationships.

The first thing is to do your research and find the celebrities that you believe represent your brand, brand values, and business. Search and see what they have been up to and what they have been saying. If you are representing a charity thinking of working with a celebrity, it is important that you do your research. Find a celebrity who has publicly spoken about your cause, or who has been affected by the issue and overall is passionate about the subject.

All this information is important when you come to pitching to their agents why you believe the said celebrity is aligned to your brand/business client(s). You need to show them the synergy, the reason to collaborate, and why their celebrity client should be working with you.

Make a list of a few celebrities as you may not always get a "yes" from the personality at the top of your list and you will need to make your way down the list.

The next step is then to track down the celebrity's agent or manager and create a relationship. You might be lucky enough to have a direct relationship with the celebrity, which is fantastic; otherwise, it is normal to go through their agent. It is important to remember that agents and managers are the doorkeepers to their celebrity clients and are being approached all the time, so you do need to try to stand out. Getting them onboard makes a difference, as they will be selling the idea to the celebrity.

There are a variety of ways to work with celebrities from turning up at your events, to endorsing your business.

Celebrity Endorsements

A celebrity endorsement provides an alternative to creative advertisements, where the celebrity endorsements tends to speak directly to the public.

Charities are known to use celebrities to promote their campaigns. There are many celebrities involved in charitable work whether as patrons or spokespeople, where they bring credibility and attention, a vital ingredient of success in a world flooded with so much noise generated by media messages. If celebrities are fully informed and engaged with the cause they are promoting, the message can really influence the process persuading people to support the cause.

Over the years I have worked with many celebrities and patrons who have supported not-for-profits and charities. Their support has made a positive difference to the work of charities from fundraising initiatives to awareness campaigns.

It is important to be mindful of how much you are intending to draw on their time and have a flexible plan with what you would ideally like them to do for you over the next three to six months. A year of activity might seem daunting for the celebrity with their own work commitments.

There are ways of maximizing the relationship with little impact on the celebrity's actual time—from getting them to sign T-shirts in advance, which you can then auction, to quotes that you can use on your website, and other promotional materials.

Brands with big budgets are able to pay for well-known celebrities from the worlds of music, sport, film, and books. Some of the famous ones of these are George Clooney for Nespresso coffee and the L'Oréal brand is known for having a host of different brand ambassadors, from Oscar-winning actress Dame Helen Mirren, to Eva Longoria and Aishwarya Rai. There is also the famous LeBron James' celebrity endorsement of Nike. Or in India the Muthoot Group, which provides financial services, signed Amitabh Bachchan, the Bollywood megastar, as its brand ambassador.

Local Dignitaries, Politicians, and Influencers

If you have a small local launch event for your business, or if you are a local charity with an annual event or campaign launch, do not forget to invite your local Mayor, your councilor, or your local government official. They are very easy to work with and great supporters, as they like to be seen supporting good local business stories and charitable events. With a little bit planning, ensuring that you invite them in ample time, as they will have busy schedules, the presence of your local dignitary can instantly raise the profile of what you are doing. Your local media will be interested, and you can also take your own photos on the day and share online.

When Things Go Wrong

Working with well-known celebrities, however, is not without risks. I am sure we can all think of at least one celebrity partnership that we know of that has not quite gone to plan. I can think of a few and remember when actress Dame Helen Mirren said that she believed that moisturizer "probably does f*** all." The moment of candor came when Dame Helen was appearing as a brand ambassador for L'Oréal on a panel at an event in the South of France. Dame Helen is the face of L'Oréal's "Age Perfect" moisturizer range, where the advertisements she appears in are not digitally enhanced, a prerequisite made by Dame Helen when she took up the role. At the time of this "incident," L'Oréal declined to comment.

Or, what about when Pepsi in 2017 included reality star and model Kendall Jenner in its advertisement, where Jenner was positioned as the peacemaker between protesters and law enforcement, at a rally alluding to the Black Lives Matter movement. The ad, in which protesters danced and smiled with a can of Pepsi, had a scene where Jenner—a white model—arrived to bridge the divide by offering a soda to a grinning police officer. The ad experienced a backlash, where the public and critics said it was not only trivializing protests, but also the killings of black people by law enforcement.

Another example is when Nike distanced itself from Lance Armstrong over his involvement in a 2012 doping scandal. The Tour de France winner lost contracts with Nike, Anheuser-Busch, Oakley, and other cycling industry sponsors.

These days' digital media means everything is far more reactive and instant. It used to be a lot easier for celebrities and for brands to not be so under the microscope. Now that pressure is amplified tenfold when a person with millions of followers makes one tiny misstep. Do think carefully before you enter into the celebrity partnership and do not get swept away by their celebrity status. As much as they are supporting you, the celebrity is getting something from the relationship too, as they are being associated to a good cause or brand, which boosts their likeability and status.

When you are not paying A-list celebrity for their endorsement or for turning up at your event and it is a relationship based on goodwill, there is always a risk that they may not turn up or decide that they no longer want to support your initiative. This is because there is no contract and they are not obligated.

The bottom line is to do as much research as possible about the celebrities you are thinking of working with, to get a feel for who they are, so you feel you are creating the right relationship for your brand.

Case Stories

I used to work on the famous Pink Ribbon Ball, an annual fundraising event for a leading UK breast cancer charity; one of the things the success of the Ball hinged on was big celebrities turning up on the night. It was a Herculean task of dealing with schedules, egos, and demands. The work would begin at least three months in advance to invite celebrities to ensure we got the date on their schedules. We would work with their agents and invite as many celebrity guests as possible, as nearer the time many agents would call to say their clients now could not make it. We would ensure that they were all looked after well on the night and had their own table and transportation to and from the event. All this would go toward next year's event, where they would want to come back again.

I also would secure a media partnership for the Ball with a leading magazine like *Hello!* or *Ok!* This was not just a big tick for the celebrity, but their agent and publicist too! This media relationship meant that both the Ball and the celebrities were captured on the night—great PR for all. My team would send out a press release to the UK pictures desks, diary reporters (who are also known as schedulers); news desks at all the various national newspapers, magazines, and TV stations; and of course, to the paparazzi. This ensured that a wall of photographers would turn up to capture the arrival of the celebrities. It always added a buzz to the event.

For a US restaurant launch, the restaurant owner invited local business leaders, the local Mayor, local food critics, and all the local media for lunch and to meet the chef. It was a coup, with fun photos that raised the profile of the restaurant. The restaurant also had created great content that was able to be shared across their social media channels and able to tag in the influencers and dignitaries that attended the event.

Local organizations in India are very good at drawing on the support of their local councilors and government officials to gain exposure and column inches (both of which are metrics often used as indicators of success). An organization doing groundbreaking work on educating rural children wanted to raise the profile of its work but had a small budget to do so. They held a colorful and special event for all the local influencers to experience the great work that they were doing. All the VIP guests were given tours of the classroom and met the children, and the children put on a short program of entertainment. The event gave everyone who attended a memorable experience within a very limited budget.

The Polaroid brand, known for its line of instant film and images, needed to be relevant again and in 2010 created a clever partnership with Lady Gaga, the global pop star, to help with its resurgence. Lady Gaga was named creative director of Polaroid and in January 2011, when I attended the Consumer Electronics Show (CES), in Las Vegas, I was fortunate to see Lady Gaga announce three new products that were developed by her.

It was a standout moment at CES, which is always very busy and full of news stories, where every brand is competing for publicity. This partnership at that time gave Polaroid the marketing muscle of Lady Gaga.

It is important to remember whoever you decide to work with whether celebrities or social media influencers there are now rules where the influencer has to clearly label their posts when they have been paid to promote the content. However, this area is still a minefield and there is no uniformity globally.

Summary

Using celebrity endorsements is not a new idea in PR or marketing; and with the rise of social media influencers, there are numerous opportunities to be had. Wherever we may be running a business in the world—China, India, Africa, or the United States—one thing we all have in common is that our stakeholders love celebrities. When famous people are seen promoting a new product or are at an event, audiences are prompted to engage with that brand. We have learnt in this chapter that one of the main things to remember as a business, when collaborating with a high-profile personality, is the relationship you develop with them. A good relationship pays PR dividends.

Along with celebrities and social media influencers, other business assets to use in your PR activities are the creation of good images, video, and blog posts. When these are incorporated into your press releases, social media activities, and websites you automatically raise your "PR bar," which is all discussed next in Chapter 5.

CHAPTER 5

Creating Content: Using Clever Photography, Video, and Blogs

How to get your story to stand out from the crowd through the use of clever photography? It is simple; begin to "think in pictures." Visuals are essential to creating content that will help your business stand out and draw in an audience. Not only do images help make text-centric content more readable, digestible, and memorable, but they can also be used to craft compelling messages that speak volumes without using a single word. Plus, good images can also strengthen your press release, as journalists recognize the power of good images to accompany a news story. However, I find that many organizations and brands always seem to forget to invest in this aspect.

Posting a photo or video online and waiting for the business offers to start rolling in is not an effective strategy. Neither is hinging your visual content success on creating the next viral phenomenon. To ensure you are positioning your visual content to deliver business results, look at what you are trying to achieve with your visual content. Remember your audience and what they want from your feed. The best visual experiences are those that find a way to tap into the power of emotion; and of course, create content that is consistent and promotes your brand value.

Along with consistent brand values, it is important to keep your visuals as brand-consistent as possible, including using your logos and colors. The best visual is when you can identify the brand it belongs to in an instant, no matter where the content appears.

Stock photographs and illustrations may save time, yet they cannot tell as compelling a story of your brand as bespoke authentic images can. If you are low on designer resources and feel that you need to turn to a stock service now and again, try to find a way to put your own branded spin on the images you select.

Do not forget you can repurpose information and adapt your popular written content into attractive visuals of charts and infographics. It is a great way to draw fresh attention to your content, helping to make your brand's insights more digestible, memorable, and shareable.

Another great way to generate content is to use your own follower content, as consumers love to snap their own pictures and share them with their friends. So, why not put their photography skills to good use by including their work in your content marketing and giving them credit. It will also strengthen engagement.

Video

Using video content in your PR and marketing efforts is an incredible way to create content that is personal and has a real impact on your audience. It has an incomparable ability to create emotion-driven sales and sales are always personal on some level. Buyers want to feel good about their choice and video marketing, when done correctly, is the best way to create this feeling. Tellingly, 92 percent of people who consume mobile videos share them with other people (Hubspot 2018); this is a big portion and is higher than the share rate of many other types of content.

So, when you use online video in your digital strategy, you have the perfect opportunity to enhance your brand's message, through simple features like design and branding, to more advanced features like voice and content; video marketing is the ideal tool to strengthen your brand identity and make sure that your customers know who you are. To make your videos as memorable as possible, ensure that you are keeping them in line with your brand strategy. This means keeping colors, fonts, logos, and voice the same in your video marketing as they are in your blogs and articles. While videos do things text content does not, users should still be able to recognize the style and format of your brand's videos online.

However, when a company's content fails to perform well on a given device or browser system, the business behind it usually loses traffic and suffers decreased conversions as a result. Fortunately, video content is fit for consumption on all devices, ranging from computers to mobile phones. This expands video's reach and makes it more user-friendly and consumer-focused.

Also, by adding video to your landing pages, website, and content offers, it is easy to improve your company's SEO (search engine optimization) value and improve your click-through rates across the board.

Livestreaming

Livestreaming has become hugely popular and dare I say a phenomenon—it is real-time online video broadcasts that are available through mobile apps, as well as on the desktop. Livestreaming gives brands the opportunity to capture events and moments as they happen, which create uniquely engaging stories to share with their audience. It is one of the most genuine ways to connect with stakeholders and allows for levels of personalization that the PR industry has never seen. Backing this up, YouTube® has said that mobile video consumption grows by 100 percent every year (Forbes 2017; www.forbes.com/sites/forbesagencycouncil/2017/02/03/video-marketing-the-future-of-content-marketing/#39be0eac6b53).

One of the main reasons you might want to consider livestreaming is simply due to its large user base and growing popularity. It has the potential to reach thousands of new customers. When tactics like SEO and content marketing are taking up too much time and money, you need a new outlet to drive traffic; using livestream platforms is a nearly free way to drive revenue for your business. In May 2016 it was predicted that video streaming market will be worth 70.05 billion U.S. dollars by 2021 (Research and Markets 2018).

It is appealing because it allows us the chance to be a creator, a presenter, and be seen by stakeholders. You can broadcast anything you are doing across the world without delay or edit. With the popularity of livestreaming continuing to rise, other more conventional social media platforms have branched out into the world of livestreaming with Facebook introducing Facebook Live and Twitter launching Periscope. One of the most popular mediums is Instagram, which in June 2018 reported that it had reached 1 billion monthly active users, up from 800 million in September 2017 (Statista 2018). The app is one of the most popular social networks worldwide.

However, while the inspiration to livestream takes its lead from reality TV and YouTube®, it is uncensored, unedited, and unrehearsed. Used in positive ways it can be a campaigning tool, creating identity, showcasing talent, and developing skills in communication. However, in spite of the clear opportunities and gratification that livestreaming presents, it is important to remember that livestreaming can be both unpredictable and hard to moderate.

Blogging

Blogging has grown into a varied form of communication, which can be short story collections, helping businesses advertise, educate customers, inform shareholders, or inspire community interactions.

The length of content is varied, and I always suggest that posts should be at the very least 500 words long. If you do write longer pieces, make sure that your long posts are easy to read and to skim. Avoid creating walls of dense text at all costs. Plus, adding an image brings your blog post to life and does better with engagement, when it is shared on social media.

There are some basic SEO skills you can apply to any blog post you publish that will help improve your search engine rankings on search engines like Google. Some things to do are:

- The more links your blog has from high-quality, popular sites, the higher Google will rank you;
- Try to have other websites link back to your website through guest posting, blog comments, or just by publishing quality content others want to mention on their own site, so Google and other search engines can reward you for being authoritative and rank your blog posts higher.
- Have a good title and the closer your title relates to keywords people are searching for, the higher your content will rank;
- Take time to research what keywords relate to your content so that, when people search for them, your website appears as one of the most relevant results. Do add keywords to the title of your blog post in the content body.
- Easier said than done, but try to publish consistently, as it will teach web crawlers to return to your site regularly and

improve your rankings over time. Publishing regular content for site visitors to enjoy also means you become a source to rely on for consistent content.

Case Stories

A professor I was working with had just published his book on geopolitics, a weighty subject, and, while he was producing great blogs and written posts, his engagement online was low. We wanted to reach a wider audience and create a relationship with possible readers. Plus, the professor had a great personality and could explain a complex subject, which would come across well in videos, so we decided to create short videos, taking geopolitics topics that were in the news and breaking them down for businesses and business leaders to understand.

The videos were filmed easily on a smartphone and we always ensured that we had the branding of the book in the background, including all the credits at the end of each video. But the unique selling point (also known as USP) was that each video was no longer than three minutes—short and snappy. The videos did not just go up on the website, but were also uploaded on to YouTube® to help push engagement, which they successfully did.

Another great example of how strong video and livestreaming can be is this example from a wonderful online community platform that connected local people to local community events, news, and businesses. The platform called Loving Local Enfield with 16,000 plus members within its Facebook group, ran on Instagram, and via its own website. People from the community post daily about things they need answering or local news. There are moderators monitoring posts and comments. To shake things up and make it fun, occasionally Loving Local would livestream from local events. They also videoed local products and produced and interviewed local businesses—helping local traders get their personality across. All the videos had three key features—fun, passion, and community!—and are very popular.

A women's network based in North London, called the Buzzing Business Club, that works both off-line and online with a global online audience does something called the "Knowledge Hub" where they live interview business experts on topics from branding, to sales, to how to present and pitch. These interviews are livestreamed on Facebook for their female business community, who can watch and ask questions in real time. This is a great way to share knowledge, build an online presence, and be engaged with your followers. It also is adding value.

A well-being event's company would do a quick "vox pop" of video content, capturing the audience as they were leaving the events, asking them how much they enjoyed the evening. Not more than five minutes long, these videos helped reflect how worthwhile the events were and also provided the opportunity to promote the next forthcoming video at the end of the video.

Finally, a women's annual international conference in India, called the Women's Economic Forum, understands the power of livestreaming and video perfectly, where the use of video also attracts speakers. All the sessions at this four-day event are livestreamed, driving global engagement.

Summary

Somethings in life are a constant, irrespective of how fast things are changing around us, and the saying, "a picture is worth a thousand words," is as true today as it ever was. No matter what industry you are in, images sell. Creating interesting content helps you find clients, which helps to grow your business. We can see from the case stories here it does not need to be complicated or difficult to do. All that is required is some planning, action, and an element of creativity, which can be fun.

The purpose of creating content is not to be underestimated, especially when using social media to promote your business with your stakeholders. Social media is where your business blogs, images, and videos come alive. However, social media for many can be daunting; in Chapter 6, I take the fear out of getting online and using social media for PR.

CHAPTER 6

Getting to Grips with Social Media

The digital revolution is one of the most exciting things to have happened to us as a species, dramatically changing how we lead our lives, how we communicate, how we influence change, and how we do business. I am a complete social media enthusiast, as it has really empowered us as businesses, opening up our worlds. It has dramatically changed the PR industry.

From presidents, prime ministers, to royalty they are all now on social media posting, particularly on Twitter and Instagram.

I think it is also important to remember that everyone on social media who is doing it well is actually self-taught, which means that it is easy to do, once you know how. There are so many different social media platforms and you will enjoy using some platforms more than others and once you get started it can be really fun and reap benefits.

There are so many businesses not using social media platforms and as a result are holding themselves back. These businesses and brands need to change their mind-sets and be open. I meet lots of different business leaders, business consultants, and entrepreneurs who are either talking to or advising businesses on how to strengthen their businesses plans and strategies, yet they have no visible online profile themselves. I always wonder how can they be advising businesses on the future, when they themselves are not part of it?!

They all have excuses of why they are not online—ranging from we do not understand it; it is for young people; we have no time; what difference will it make. Well, if you are not online how will your customers find you, and you can bet, while you are not online, your competitor will be.

We have evolved from ink and quill, from typewriter to now the use of e-mails, blogs, and social media posts. Whatever happens we are not going back to ink and quill, so it is important to get online. The next generations are already there and are your potential future customers, clients, and business leaders; to survive and to be relevant you need to be online and active.

To help you to change your thinking, I strongly urge you to go online and watch what I consider to be one of the best video overviews of social media trends with their data sources, which is produced annually by *Socialnomics*, a movement created by Erik Qualman's number one international bestseller of the same title (https://socialnomics.net/).

Social media channels are free to use and here are some real facts to get you thinking of the value of social media for your business/organization:

- Over half the world's population is under 30 years old (UNESCO; http://unesco.org/new/en/unesco/events/prizes-and-celebrations/celebrations/international-days/world-radio-day-2013/statistics-on-youth/).
- If Facebook were a nation, it would be the top in terms of world population (SmartInsights 2019; www.smartinsights.com/social-media-marketing/social-media-strategy/new-global-social-media-research/).
- Fifty-three percent of millennials would rather lose their senses of smell than their technology (McCann research as reported in *Time* magazine 2011).
- Two-thirds of American adults get their news from social media (Pew Research 2018; www.journalism.org/2018/09/10/news-use-across-social-media-platforms-2018/).
- People will soon trust Amazon more than their bank (RFI Group 2018, the United Kingdom; www.rfigroup.com/rfi-group/news/uk-press-release-amazon-and-paypal-more-trusted-among-younger-generation-banks-hold-their).
- Ninety-three percent of buying decisions are influenced by social media (Podium 2017; http://learn.podium.com/rs/841-BRM-380/images/2017-SOOR-Infographic.jpg).
- More people own a mobile phone than a toothbrush (Mobile Marketing Association Asia; www.mmaglobal.com/research).
- The fastest growing demographic on Twitter is grandparents (globalwebindex; https://blog.globalwebindex.com/chart-of-the-day/twitter-now-the-fastest-growing-social-platform-in-the-world/).

- The LinkedIn age limit has been reduced to 13 (LinkedIn; https://blog.linkedin.com/2013/08/19/updates-to-linkedins-terms-of-service).
- The #1 used hashtag is #Love (TopHashTags.com; www.top-hashtags.com).

There are many social media platforms and I recommend finding the ones that work for you, but at the same time suggest that you are working on what I view are the key ones; and that means being active on all of them simultaneously—Twitter, Facebook, Instagram, YouTube®, and LinkedIn. We need to be engaged on each, as each platform attracts a different age group, which means that you are casting a much wider network to attract customers and an audience.

To get the most of your social media activity there are a few things you need to do, to ensure that you reap the maximum benefits. They are:

1. There are lots of moving parts to consider when writing for social media. You need to decide on platform-specific tools, such as emojis, images, GIFs, memes, and hashtags. If you are looking to tap into a millennial audience for example, you might want to consider embracing these elements, as well as common abbreviations. Do your research before making this decision; moving content tends to attract more engagement.
2. Make all your branding consistent; so when people click and see you on Twitter, Facebook, Instagram, and so on, they immediately recognize your logo and brand.
3. Include all your contact details so people can get in touch if needed. If you are online, then there is no need to hide.
4. Make sure all your posts are *authentic*; while there may be a screen between you and the world, people can sniff out anything that does not seem to be honest.

It is important to note that there is a certain etiquette about being online and I always describe it as being at a dinner party, where you want to be a good guest and be invited back again. Make sure you are listening, engaging with people, and not talking *at* people. Social media marketing is not about talking at people—it is about creating good conversations.

Always share the love online by retweeting others' posts on Twitter, sharing content that you like and tagging others in, who you know will also enjoy the content. Paying it forward online grows your own following and helps your brand reach a bigger community and bandwidth.

As a rule of thumb—and one that works for us whatever age we might be—do not share anything that you would not want your parents to read. That way you always keep it clean.

You cannot control social media, so be brave. Being online is very serendipitous, where you can create lots of business opportunities without knowing where they may come from (see Chapter 12).

Once you start broadcasting on social media, you need to turn up every day. It is like being an actor at the theatre; you need to turn up for your show as your audience expects it. If you are unreliable, people will lose interest in you, your brand, and that affects your following.

Your collective social media following on all your channels is something called your "social media capital," and this has a value. There have been many times when I have been speaking to the media, whether they are based in the United Kingdom, the United States, or South Africa, where I have been asked, "What is the social worth of your client." Why? Because the media also want to attract new readers and if you can bring more people to their magazine or online platform then you will be of immediate interest.

Case Stories

A small family-run business working with people with learning difficulties was doing strong work around the world, but found they were not attracting the clients they should be and as a result their business was not thriving. Their social media activity and engagement was virtually nonexistent and acknowledged they had to turn things around; they had shifted their mind-set.

Another story that predates Instagram is about a professor at a leading global business school, who had just written his new book and wanted to raise both his book and his own profile. He created a Twitter account, started tweeting daily, tagging in relevant journalists, the media, and influencers. Within three months he had been invited to speak abroad based on the topic of his book, was interviewed twice by the BBC, and boosted book sales.

Another author, who was a business consultant, had a zero social media profile, but he got active and engaged online, tagging current clients and companies that he would like to work with, and started to win new business based on the content of his book that he was sharing, without reducing the value of the book.

Key Performance Indicators (KPIs)

Social media marketing is a fundamental part of any business. It drives sales and those businesses that focus on building their social media engagement benefit from a strong PR reach, which generates greater brand awareness, which ultimately makes it easier to attract new customers.

Businesses need to understand the success of their online activities and what is working for them and, to do this, they need to measure their social media key performance indicators (KPIs). Tracking KPIs improves your online PR and marketing strategy. However, it is important to recognize that we do not all measure the same things or measure the same ways, or use the same tools or terminology. To help us all be more aligned, we need to understand exactly what we mean when we use or say certain words in measuring our activities.

So, with this in mind, I recommend *the Dictionary of Public Relations Measurement and Research* (Stacks and Bowen 2013), which has become one of the most popular papers the Institute for Public Relations has ever published! Visitors can download the dictionary for free (https://instituteforpr. org/dictionary-public-relations-measurement-research-third-edition/).

Otherwise, to get started, there are four core social media KPIs that I strongly suggest businesses and organizations focus on and they are:

1. *Engagement*: Reaching lots of people means nothing if they are not interested in what you have to offer. Low engagement means that either your content is not resonating with your stakeholders or that your marketing message is weak. The actual KPIs that you as a business can measure for engagement are the numbers of click, likes, shares, comments, brand mentions, profile visits, and active

followers. This data will give you an insight into what kind of content your stakeholders enjoy.

2. *Reach*: Indicates how far your message is traveling, which you can measure by tracking the KPIs of total number of followers; impressions, which show how many times your post showed up in someone's newsfeed or timeline, either because they are already following you or because someone they know has liked or shared your content; and traffic data, which is the traffic to your website. If you are putting a lot of time and effort into your social media content, then you will want to see that this is reflected to the traffic to your website.

3. *Leads*: Once your social media accounts start to gain traction, it is important to find out how many of these engaged stakeholders are actually interested in making a purchase from your business. To answer this, you will need to measure lead generation from social media and, if you are not generating leads, you may be on the wrong platform or your content is not attracting your desired stakeholder. Therefore, the sooner you start to track to find out, the better.

4. *Conversions*: The ultimate measurement of your success in social media marketing is if you have found the right people, kept them engaged, and who are interested to buy from you.

Based on the foregoing discussion, we will look at each of several important social media platforms individually to better understand how they can be used and how they are evaluated.

Instagram

Right at the start, Instagram was created as an app and has quickly become a powerful marketing tool for businesses looking to expand their presence and the visibility of their products. This is a fairly new platform, launched in October 2010, and is evolving with a greater emphasis on making money through product placement. Its latest program, called "shoppable posts," allows businesses to add "tags" to the products in their photos with links that include a product description, price, and the ability to "shop now," which will lead the user to their online stores. This service is simple for a business to attract actual sales from the site and 72 percent of

Instagram users admit to purchasing products through the social media platform (Business Insider 2017).

You will need to approach it as a *curated visual experience* that showcases your brand, which needs to be both creatively presented and strategically planned if you want to build a strong relationship with your audience. You should use Instagram hashtags (e.g., #theprknowledgebook) to help place your content and products in front of the right people.

For example, if your brand's target market is female entrepreneurs, you will want to start thinking about what kind of content resonates with this stakeholder group and you could post about women in business and entrepreneurship, or write blog posts about marketing and branding, thus empowering females in the workplace. These topics will influence what kind of hashtags you will want to use for individual post; when it comes to choosing your hashtags, it is important not to be generic. You might think using the "#entrepreneur" hashtag is a good one. But that would be mistaken, as this hashtag has nearly *40 million posts* under it, which is updated every couple of seconds. This means the results are too broad, the market is saturated, and means you run the risk of your post getting lost in all that noise. Instead, find hashtags that are more streamlined and targeted to your audience, such as #womenentrepreneur, which is specific to female entrepreneurs and more likely to reach your target group of stakeholders.

To find suitable hashtags go into "Instagram's Explore page," and search for a hashtag that you know would work for your brand and messaging. When Instagram produces the results under that hashtag, it also gives you a scroll bar at the top of related hashtags. This is a great place to find new hashtags for your posts. Remember to check how many posts have been published under the hashtag you have chosen; if it has been used thousands of times, it could be too saturated, and your posts will probably go unseen.

When you are running a small business, time is restricted and, as you will not be able to dedicate your days to Instagram marketing, you will need to stay organized and plan ahead to have the most success. With this is in mind, I suggest posting at least four to five times a week. Look at your analytics, which will show which days and dates are popular for you to post. Decide which KPIs you will use to base your decisions regarding success or failure or improvement. By simple planning and creating an editorial calendar for your Instagram profile, you will be able to build a more balanced relationship between strategy and art into your feed.

Instagram Analytics

Instagram provides for free insights to help you learn more about your followers and the people interacting with your business on Instagram. For example, you will find insights such as gender, age range, and location. You can also see which posts and stories your audience sees and engages with the most—depending of course on which KPIs you think are most important. Insights and metrics about your account should include *paid* as well as *placed* or *owned* activity. KPIs such as reach, accounts reached, impressions, and impressions by day reflect both paid and organic activity.

To access this, you need to convert your profile to a business profile, where the insight can be accessed. Here you can select specific posts, stories, or promotions you would like to view data and you can also learn more about your audience.

In Instagram analysis the website Activity tab allows you to track weekly interactions, reach, and impressions. The Content tab lets you see how your posts, stories, and promotions are performing, while the Audience tab gives important insights on your stakeholder groups.

Instagram Suggestions to Follow

Following are my top three favorite influencers on Instagram who I feel I learn from, as their curation of posts is clever and because I believe we can learn from people around the world:

- Huda Kattan—@hudabeauty—is an Iraqi-American makeup artist, beauty blogger, and entrepreneur, and founder of the cosmetics line Huda Beauty.
- Vishakha Vij—@theurbanelog—is based in India, who is an influencer, a content creator, and a lifestyle and beauty blogger.
- Joel Contartese—@joelcontartese—is one of the first entrepreneurs to monetize social media in 2012. On his official website, Joel says he believes "connecting people is the most valuable and misunderstood element of business" (http://joelcontartese.wpengine.com/my-story/).

Facebook Business Page

A Facebook Page is another platform that allows businesses to develop their brand, grow their audience, and start conversations with customers and people interested in learning more. To create a Facebook Page, you will need to already have a personal profile, as only people with profiles on Facebook can create or have a role on Pages.

It is free to create a Page for your business, and all you need to do is follow the steps for creating a Page and decide how you would like to use your Page to interact with people and customers on Facebook. Once your Page is created, you can get access to free features, from Page Insights, publishing tools, and others that help you manage your Page.

Like Instagram, you need to create an online presence for your business, which will help build social connections with your audience and drive real business results. Again, it is about curating the tone, style, and personality of your business.

Posts with images do better on Facebook and you can showcase your brand through photos and video. Plus, putting a face to your business through a Facebook Page reminds your audience that it is run by real people and is authentic.

The platform also helps you engage in one-to-one conversations through comments and messaging.

Facebook ads can be a way to grow your brand and audience that is not expensive to use. You are in control and can choose where you place your ads, your target audience, budget, and schedule. You will have access to other Facebook advertising tools to help you understand what you are getting in return from each ad you run.

Facebook offers many tools to connect with the different communities that you care about via profile, pages, groups, and events.

Facebook Page Analytics

I suggest posting at least once to twice a week to keep your Facebook Page active. Understanding your Facebook page's KPI metrics gives you the information you need to make sure you are putting the right content in front of the right audience. It helps you work with Facebook's algorithm instead of just sending content into the void and hoping someone will see it.

Facebook also sends you weekly statistics to show you how your posts are doing, and you can also click into your actual Facebook Page and click "insights," which tracks three important measurements:

- *Page Likes*: How many people liked your page over the last seven days, where each of your new likes came from, such as from visiting your page directly, or from a page suggestion, or from mobile or desktop.
- *Post Reach*: How many people saw all the content you posted over the last seven days, which gives you an overview of how many people saw content from your page and how they interacted with it.
- *Engagement*: How many people liked, shared, or commented on your posts over the last seven days.

Facebook Pages Suggestions to Follow

Here are my top Facebook Pages that keep me fresh and inspired:

- Mari Smith—a top marketing expert and one of the first people I followed on social media (https://facebook.com/marismith/).
- Kim Garst—a Forbes Top 10 Women Social Media Influencer and CEO of Boom Social (https://facebook.com/kimgarstbiz/).
- Chris Brogan—a business advisor and a *New York Times* best-selling author. I also had the pleasure to meet Chris who is a firm believer in serendipity (https://facebook.com/broganchris).

Twitter

Twitter is perhaps my favorite social media platform, because I enjoy the way it can randomly connect you to people and everything is in real time. I find it serendipitous and fun; like Instagram and Facebook, it drives engagement for your brand and is about being active. Here are some of the things you need to know to get started and to get the most out of the platform.

- Ideally, you want to be on Twitter 15 minutes a day, at different times in the day because people from around the world come on to the platform in real time. I suggest splitting your 15 minutes into five minutes in the morning, five minutes at lunchtime, and then again in the afternoon/evening.
- Twitter has established itself as a news platform, where in real time it shows you what topics and news are trending; these days breaking news is broken first on this platform before it has been released on leading news networks such as CNN or the BBC.
- Next there is your Twitter handle, which is the name people give themselves on Twitter—@username.
- Twitter has its quirks, and is all about brief communications where you can only send out your message, which is called a "Tweet" that is made up of 280 characters. Your tweets can include a link to any web content (blog post, website page, PDF document, and so forth) or a photograph or video.
- People follow and subscribe to your Twitter account and you follow other people. This allows you to read, reply to, and easily share their tweets with your followers, which is called a "retweet," or "retweeting." Importantly, your content does not have to be solely branded and you can share other content by sourcing it from relevant industry news, blog posts, newspaper articles, and so forth. Identify the news and publications that are most relevant to your industry. Set up alerts for these sources and for the hot topics of your industry and take a look at your timeline to see what everyone else is talking about.
- Creating lists is the easiest way to see what your followers are tweeting. So, if you have some major influencers in the food industry, then add them to a private list.
- Make sure people know who you are, what you are selling, and how to buy it. You can put your shop link into your bio or pin it to the top of your profile page.
- Again, this is a platform that uses hashtags. Twitter makes it easy to expand your audience reach using #hashtags. This is because people who are following #hashtags can find you, even if they are not your followers.

- You can always schedule your tweets. Again, there are tools that will do it all for you, plus they can tell you when your community is most active. Just be careful to keep an eye on them, so you can jump in if anything needs changing in the interim.
- Shorten your links. As mentioned, Twitter is known for its bitesize posts. If you want to pack as much into your tweets as possible, shortening links help you go that extra mile. Bitly, HootSuite, and Buffer will do this for you.
- Find influencers. It is vital to start talking to the right people to turbocharge your marketing efforts. That means reaching out to industry influencers, so you get to piggyback on their huge followings. Just remember, half of Twitter users say they rely on influencers for product recommendations.

Twitter Insights and Analytics

Twitter's analytics help you understand how the content you share on Twitter grows your business. Your "Account home" features high-level KPI statistics tracked from month to month and highlights your top-performing Tweets and introduces you to the influencers in your network, people that you should be following.

- *Tweet Activity Dashboard*: This is a rich source of KPI metrics for every single one of your Tweets. You will know exactly how many times Twitter users have seen, retweeted, liked, and replied to each Tweet.
- *Audience Insights Dashboard*: This graphic and textual dashboard contains valuable information about the people who follow you on Twitter, where you can track your follower growth over time, and learn more about their interests and demographics.

Twitter Suggestions to Follow

There are so many people that I could recommend to follow here on Twitter, keeping with Twitter's randomness here are my eclectic three:

- Thomas Power—@thomaspower—an entrepreneur, a business advisor, and a professional speaker on social media, technology, and the world of digital.
- Malala Yousafzai—@Malala—a Pakistani activist for female education and the youngest Nobel Prize laureate.
- Marie Forleo—@marieforleo—an American life coach, motivational speaker, author, and web television host of Marie TV with a focus on small business and personal development training for entrepreneurs. She is the owner of Marie Forleo International and B-School.

LinkedIn

According to LinkedIn editor Daniel Roth (2018), every day, over 2 million posts, videos, and articles course through the LinkedIn feed, generating tens of thousands of comments every hour—and tens of millions more shares and likes. It is one of the best networking tools for business owners and job seekers and, by using a LinkedIn business page, you can attract top talent, position yourself as a thought-leader in your industry, and promote your products or services. One of the things to think about doing on LinkedIn is to create a *company page*, which will help potential customers learn about your business, brand, products, services, and job opportunities.

Company Page

Creating a LinkedIn company page is easy and similar to the Facebook Page, where you will need a personal LinkedIn account and a verified e-mail address. LinkedIn guides you through the process of setting up a company page and, if you have questions, you can always visit LinkedIn's help page.

Once created, you can start editing your company page; LinkedIn requires that you include a company description, which should be information about your business, such as what products and services you offer, your company's history, and its mission.

After crafting your company description, fill in other company details, such as your website, where you are headquartered, company type, company size, and your company's specialties. Make sure you upload your company logo and cover image before hitting publish.

If you have a team, let them know the page is active so they can edit their position description and add the company page to their personal accounts.

LinkedIn Groups

LinkedIn Groups are great places to build an engaged community surrounding your business and to grow your online community. There are so many groups that you can join on LinkedIn that will fit your interests, from public relations to branding, to publishing, to films and media, to women in business, to blockchain, to fashion, and more! You can also join groups based on location, a good way to enter a new location that you have been thinking of by being active in that group. Or, you can also create your own group. Either way, being active in LinkedIn Groups will establish you as a thought-leader and an industry expert. It also sends more people to your company's LinkedIn page.

However, LinkedIn Groups are not a place to share ads for your business; instead, share valuable content with people who are interested in your business and industry. It is about creating meaningful conversations. Once you have created a company page, career page, and LinkedIn Group, regularly use these assets and create content for them. Here are some tips on where to get started and how to build these pages:

1. *Followers:* Publishing and sharing content is pointless if no one is seeing it. You should be constantly looking for new followers on LinkedIn. You can post a widget to your LinkedIn page on your website and add your LinkedIn information to your e-mail signature. In fact, you should be adding all your social media information to your signature—Twitter, Facebook Page, and Instagram. So, people can find you and follow.

2. *Publish and Share Relevant Content:* As with any successful marketing campaign, you need to know who your stakeholders are and what they want to see on LinkedIn. It is important to publish and share content that benefits your followers—not just content that promotes your company.

3. *Do Not Be Overly Self-Promotional*: Instead, you want to provide content that is helpful, informative, and interesting. Your followers will be put off with constant marketing messages. No one likes to be sold to or see commercials all the time.

4. *Vary What You Post*: Seeing the same thing repeatedly gets boring and annoying. Make posts a mix of visual, video, and regular articles.

5. *Experiment with Video and Photos*: LinkedIn has a video and photo feature. In 2018, it introduced filters and a couple of text styles to its video feature; the filters include "Work High Five," "Side Hustle," and "On the Air."

6. *Sponsored Ads*: Like other social media platforms, you can create sponsored ads on LinkedIn, but they do cost money. There is freedom and customization available with this feature, where you can select the geographic range you want your ad to target, the ages of the audience you're seeking, the profession and industries of the stakeholders you are seeking, and more.

LinkedIn Tracking and Analytics

The best way to offer relevant content to your audience is knowing what they want by monitoring and tracking past posts. You will determine what works and what does not. LinkedIn's Company Page analytics allows you to evaluate KPIs such as engagement on your posts, identify trends, understand your follower demographics, and learn more about your page traffic.

LinkedIn Top Voices

LinkedIn also does something called "Top Voices," which is a global annual list of influencers on the platform, where its editors bring their data scientists together to sort through various articles and updates that spanned over the past year.

Again, there are so many Top Voices that I could recommend, but my personal favorites are these three, mainly because I know two of them and have seen them become the superstars they are:

- Sanyin Siang. CEO coach, professor, and author. Siang, who is an engineering professor at Duke and executive director of the Fuqua/Coach K Center on Leadership & Ethics, talks about behavioral science principles and then focuses on the human factors. She tries to engage different perspectives in her video conversations and enjoys experimenting with different formats, such as travelogues.

- Prof. Jonathan A.J. Wilson PhD. Academic, consultant, and author. Wilson specializes in business and culture. He is an international speaker and author of the book, *Halal Branding*.
- Richard Branson. Founder, Virgin Group. Branson is Britain's well-known entrepreneur and businessman, who covers all aspects of his life and work, from his travel adventures to the initiatives of Virgin Group's more than 60 companies in his LinkedIn feed. Branson says, "I don't see any separation between and work and play—it's all just living, and I love sharing all of it" (post published by Branson, 2018, on Virgin.com).

YouTube®

As we now know from the previous chapter, video is key, and it makes sense to be here as a business. Just like any other social network, it is free and YouTube® represents a community and is specifically designed for uploading and sharing video content.

It is important to understand who the YouTube® user is, as they are much younger than those on other platforms along with some clear trends. Understanding what these are can help you to create content that will appeal to your target audience:

- *Mobile*: Users are consuming content on the go; according to YouTube®, 70 percent of time spent watching videos on the site comes from mobile devices (source: YouTube® at www.youtube.com/intl/en-GB/yt/about/press/).
- *Millennial*: While YouTube® attracts users of all age groups, a large proportion of this age bracket visit the site. Millennials are defined as people born between 1981 and 1996, according to the Pew Research Center (www.pewresearch.org/topics/millennials/).

- *Global*: Available in 80 languages and offering 91 local versions (www.youtube.com/intl/en-GB/yt/about/press/).

People use it to watch videos and visual content from brands, as well as other users. It is this user-generated content that YouTube® is particularly well-known for; while the average user may see it as a means of accessing entertainment and visual content, the site represents another platform for businesses to incorporate into their social media strategy. Some of the most popular categories on YouTube are:

- Beauty
- Comedy
- Gaming
- Music
- Sports

To get started on YouTube®, you are going to need a Google account, where you can either create a new, dedicated account specifically for your YouTube® business channel or use an existing, personal account. Once you have created a channel for your business, you will need to brand your channel, which includes:

1. *Branding*: Your channel icon and banner are both opportunities to promote your business. Displaying your logo and images of your products can keep viewers curious and help you make a name for yourself.
2. *Description*: This section offers more information about your organization, such as what you do and why.
3. *Links*: They provide the opportunity for you to include links to your business' website and other social media sites, such as Facebook, Instagram, and Twitter.
4. *Activity*: Like any other social media site, be an active member of the community that your business is trying to reach. Signaling yourself as an active participant in the community means following other channels, liking other videos, and letting your viewers know that you are involved in your industry. Highlighting featured channels and "liked"

videos is a subtle way to show your fellow YouTube® creators support. It is a smart strategy to make your YouTube® business channel appear more active, if you do not plan on uploading on a frequent basis.

5. *YouTube Business Account/Brand Account*: You can add owners and managers, giving you the option of letting multiple team members have access to your account. Owners have full access to the channel, while managers can use the channel for admin purposes on behalf of the owners.

6. *As a Small Business, You Will Need to Create Your Video Content Yourself*. The quality of the videos you produce depends a lot on the equipment you are using; ensure that your devices are up-to-date and have the right camera and video settings for filming content. Make sure you include branding within your video.

There are two things to be aware of when using YouTube® and they are:

1. There is advertising on the YouTube® platform, and ads will be appearing alongside your videos; you cannot control which ads are displayed. Also, YouTube® decides which related content to show users, meaning you have little control over which ads and videos are displayed with your company's content.

2. Unless you opt to restrict comments, users will be able to leave reviews directly beneath your video; these reviews will impact on your KPIs. Your business will not be able to manage what they say and how they say it, meaning your video comments section could end up filled with negative reviews or online arguments.

YouTube Analytics

In your channel homepage, there is a tab called "Views," which takes you to the analytics, where you can see how your videos are performing based on a number of KPIs. The "overview" report in analytics will show data for the past 28 days, which can be altered to show different time periods.

- *Annotations*: These are links in the video that people can click on to be taken to other pages you want them to find. Learn which annotations people click on and the result of this action. Key performance indicators include:

1. *Audience Retention*—tells you how long people watch your videos, before leaving the page.
2. *YouTube® Cards*—is a graphic at the end of a YouTube® video that encourages viewers to explore more content or directs stakeholders and other audiences to take a specific action. If users subscribe to your YouTube® channel, they will be alerted whenever you upload new content. Cards can be monitored to see which ones users are interacting the most.
3. *Comments*—assess the statistics around the number of comments and how often your videos receive them and do manage replies to comments.
4. *Demographics*—discover who is watching your videos, including data on age and geographical location.
5. *Devices*—allow you to see what people are watching your content on, such as mobile or desktop.
6. *Sharing*—provides you with which social media networks your videos have been shared on, and how many times, and how many likes (shown as a thumbs up, 👍)/dislikes (shown as a thumbs down, 👎) you have per video.
7. *Playback locations*—with this report, you can discover which websites your videos are watched on, whether they are on YouTube® itself, another page you are linked to, or pages where your videos are embedded.
8. *Subscribers*—find out which videos are most and the least likely to get people to subscribe to your channel.
9. *Traffic sources*—this report lets you discover how people are finding your videos, such as by searching for it, or being referred from your website, social media sites, or other pages.
10. *Videos in playlist*—view which of your videos have been added to playlists.
11. *Views*—collect data on how many times your videos are viewed, which is good for measurement of stakeholder penetration.

YouTube® Suggestions to Follow

The Stanford Graduate Business School allows viewers to step inside the classroom via their YouTube® channel and experience interviews with big influencers and business classes taught by renowned scholars (https://www.youtube.com/channel/UCGwuxdEeCf0TIA2RbPOj-8g).

The Google Small Business channel features advice from experts on how to get your small business noticed online and offers a variety of channels based on your area of expertise (https://youtube.com/user/GoogleBusiness/featured).

The Harvard Business Review channel gathers all online and print content into one place with topics ranging from business leadership to current news (https://youtube.com/user/HarvardBusiness/featured).

The Last Word About Social Media

It may be impossible for you to be on all the platforms, but if you can do four make it: Twitter, LinkedIn, Instagram, and YouTube®. Remember to have fun with it and be open to connect with people, as you just do not know who people know within their own circles and feeds—remember it is all about your mind-set.

Finally, learn from the next generation, whether they are your kids, nephews, or nieces. This next generation understands better than us, of how things work and how to engage. Some of my best Instagram lessons of "how to" have come from our 12-year-old!

Podcasts

Before we leave this chapter, I want to mention podcasts, which have been proven to be extremely popular in 2018, especially with young listeners, who are more likely to use podcasts to discover news rather than listening to the radio (Podcasts Insights.com, 2019). A podcast is an audio file similar to a radio broadcast, without the commercial breaks, and is available to stream online for listeners. Once your audience members have found you based on your specific content, they can subscribe to your channel. When you upload new content, it will automatically download to their devices. They are relatively easy and inexpensive to make.

Podcasts offer opportunities for audiences to share in-depth discussions and incredible real-life stories. As a business owner, you want to build your credibility and your authority on your platform; podcasting is a great way to do this—share your knowledge and position yourself as an expert in your field. You will need to make your audience understand the amount of value that you can bring to their lives and businesses. If you deliver high quality, you are building trust, credibility, reputation, relationship, and authority.

Now is the time to build on that popularity, focusing on podcasts as a source with fresh, interesting content, where you can interview guests to strengthen your content. When you are starting a business, or even if your business is established, connecting with influencers is an asset. It is your chance to connect, exchange, share opinions, and sometimes even share some valuable information. It is a first step to various collaborations with those guests. Getting in touch with influencers can be done during live events, via e-mail, on their blogs by adding comments regularly, or via social media (see Chapter 4 on working with influencers and celebrities). These collaborations could lead to joint ventures, products creation, online summits, speaking engagements, and guest blogging.

Podcasting is a medium that can be accessed while your stakeholders are on the go—travelling to work, going to meetings, at the gym, on the school run—wherever they are listening, the experience is that it feels as though you are part of a conversation. It is intimate. Therefore, it is important to be authentic and speak with your heart, as the way you communicate with people is the way they will perceive who you are and what your brand is like.

Talking is extremely powerful and being listened to is even more powerful. As a small business, or organization or being self-employed, you can look to build awareness and engage a new audience.

Case Stories

A small, global publishing house that publishes business books creates podcasts by interviewing its different authors, who share their knowledge and wisdom for the business community.

A life coach does a monthly podcast, interviewing other therapists and coaches whether they are nutritionists, dream analysts, and wellbeing experts. It has positioned him as an expert in his field and grown his audience and client base.

Summary

After reading this chapter and absorbing all the facts, there is little doubt that social media is one of the most empowering mediums to have evolved for all types of businesses. The key is not to be overwhelmed and think of it as another task to do in your busy business day, but instead to approach your social media activities as part of your business strategy. Investing in your social media PR plans and measuring your KPIs means you will not only be raising the profile of your brand with your stakeholders, but you could actually be making sales.

Probably, one of the best things social media can do for a small organization or business is open up your business to a whole new world, which is not on your doorstep. In one clever social media swoop, by taking the data from your KPIs, you could be engaging with new stakeholders in Hong Kong, Dubai, Barbados, Mumbai, Ghana, and more, where the world is really your oyster. All you need is a global frame of mind, so let's discover what this means and how to get going in the next chapter.

CHAPTER 7

Small, Medium-sized Businesses (SMEs) Need a Global Mind-set

I have been looking forward to writing this chapter because I have witnessed and experienced the opportunities out there for small businesses and the self-employed. We are living in the realms of the World Wide Web, which gives any and every small business the opportunity to be global. To be able to cash in on these opportunities, small, medium-sized businesses (SMEs) need to have a global mind-set and be relevant in today's world and be ready to sell worldwide. There are a whole host of prospects and doing business around the world can seem a long way from doing business in your hometown; yet each year countless small businesses enter new markets. Entering the international arena can protect you against the risk of decline in domestic markets and, importantly, can significantly improve your overall growth potential.

Going Global

By tweaking your brand story, service, and products to interest your international target audience, SMEs can be global without leaving their desks. There are certain things to think about before you jump in and, since PR is based on communications between people, you need to pay attention to cultural differences, where the most obvious ones are:

- *Market Research*—For every single country or region that you wish to enter, start with local research to help determine whether to enter that local market or not. A few questions to ask yourself are:

1. Is your target market familiar with your product or service?
2. How many potential users are there?
3. What do these users currently rely on?
4. Will your current business model work?
5. How will you handle support for local customers?
6. Are you legally authorized to bring your product, use your brand name, hire the needed people, and monetize it?

Tip: You can use your own Facebook Page to gain insights, by narrowing down your audience to a specific country. This is a great way to get insights from locals who already know your product. You need to really understand the local market, their habits, how they use the web and mobile, if and how they buy online, and how they engage with products like yours.

- *Local Competition*—Understand who the other players are and find out:
  1. Who is your competitor in this region?
  2. What do they offer?
  3. What are they good at and what are their weaknesses?
  4. What do people say about them both online and off-line?
- *Local Knowledge*—Doing some groundwork could save you resources and embarrassments. Understand what kind of systems locals use. For example, understand their metric systems, if you are selling items with weight, as in some countries people do not know what "pounds" are and use "kilograms" instead. Other factors to consider are currencies and do not forget that dates are formatted differently, too. Colors can mean different things, too. In most markets, green means growth and indicates an upward trend, while red means the opposite. In South Korea and China, red signifies an upward trend.
- *Evaluate and Select Methods of How You Will Distribute Your Product Abroad*—You can choose from a variety of means for distributing your product, from opening company-owned foreign subsidiaries to working with agents, representatives, and distributors, and setting up joint ventures.

- *Understand How to Set Prices, Negotiate Deals, and Navigate the Legal Quagmire When Exporting*—Make sure you package and label each in accordance with regulations in the market you are selling to and the globalization of transportation systems helps here, but regulations are still different everywhere you go.
- *The Web and Social Media in Other Countries*—Not all countries use Google and in places such as China and Russia they have alternatives—Yandex (in Russia) or Baidu (used in China). Also, make sure to identify the correct keywords and topics. Cultural differences can affect your posts, too, the type of questions asked, tone, and images.

Tools and Ideas

To help you forge ahead into a brave new world there are lots of things to help you and are free to use:

- *Google's Market Finder*—This is a great tool to use for western markets, which will not only help you identify the best markets for your product or service, but also will tell you how to prepare for them, as Market Finder can deliver key insights, such as the disposable income of potential customers and their Internet behavior. It will also help you navigate areas like localization, international payments, and logistics. It can also help strengthen advertising by identifying the appropriate language to use, the best way to reach customers, and the right devices to target.
- *LinkedIn Groups*—Do not forget to use LinkedIn Groups that are active in the regions that you are thinking of working in and are a great way to create relationships and find out what is happening locally. When I was attending CES in 2011, which is annually hosted in Las Vegas, I wanted to find local business, PR, and marketing groups. I searched on LinkedIn for relevant groups based in Las Vegas and posted in them that I was going to be at CES and welcomed the opportunity to have coffee with people who wanted to network with a

London publicist. From those posts I made some solid connections (many of whom are now close business connections), which has also led to collaborations and work overtime.

- *International Trade Events and Conferences*—If you have the resources, do think about attending industry events in the regions that you want to go global in, as not only will you make connections, but you will gain an insight into the local market.
- *Writing for International Platforms*—If you have a book or are an expert in a particular sector, think about writing for news platforms in the areas that you want to enter. This will help raise your profile locally, build an affinity with the area, and start to ground you as an expert within that region.
- *International Places Have Local Media*—Once you get going in an international region that you have broken into, remember that this place will have local media who could be interested in your story.

Case Stories

I think this story is a great example of a small entrepreneur working global. I met a female jewelry maker in Delhi, India, who is Israeli and lives in Israel, but she has a passion for India and a love for its fashion and jewelry. She has turned her passion into a business, where she visits India to create stunning jewelry with local Indian artisans, which she then sells globally via Instagram. Her brand on Instagram is @elfasihayajewelry.

A high-end UK beach brand called Kaneshka (now rebranded to Kaminee) wanted to enter the Caribbean market, specifically Barbados. One of the ways they got their brand before the boutiques they wanted to be stocked in was to send an item to each boutique buyer. Being a small island there were not many boutiques on their list and therefore was within their marketing budget. For them it was worth taking the risk to send their products, as they wanted the boutiques to feel the quality of their garments. They had identified Barbados as the perfect market for them and where they envisioned their brand.

A great story of purpose is one where a business book author based in Japan wanted to enter the Indian market with his book and one of the ways we did this was to acquire for him the opening to write for an influential online Indian news platform who would then include his byline and link to the book.

A female American entrepreneur wanted to do more international work and wanted to travel, so she created opportunities for herself to speak in global locations that she wanted to be in and open doors for herself. This not only grew her network but also led to other offerings.

Creating collaborations with local businesses in the areas that you want to enter is another great way to going global. These should be partnerships where you add value to your brand and can be with partners outside your sector. A UK life coach business wanted to take their work into the south of India, so they contacted spas and retreats in this part of the world with the idea to collaborate. They are now running sessions in South India regularly and expanding their brand.

The Pitfalls

Like with anything there can be challenges of going global, from chasing too many opportunities to getting stung by currency fluctuations. The game of international expansion has threats that domestic-only business people never see; and small businesses can be particularly vulnerable to problems. Some of these can be avoided by planning your strategy instead of chasing inquiries the world over. Just because dozens of countries showed interest does not mean you are ready to market your product everywhere. Patience is key. You will need to tailor your sales and marketing efforts to each country.

Do not ignore the cultural differences that shape the marketplace, such as assuming business will be done in English. Familiarize yourself with the local language. Many publishers and blogs find it difficult going global because they require massive translations.

Remember, the only way to become truly global is to make sure you are truly local everywhere you go. But most of all it is about building and creating relationships with people.

Summary

From this chapter it is clear that having a global mind-set is becoming more important, particularly for small businesses and entrepreneurs, and especially as the world becomes more interconnected and as we strengthen our online business activities. It pushes us to look at things from a different perspective, which we may not have previously considered, challenging our existing outlooks.

One of the fascinating elements of having a global mind-set for entrepreneurs is looking at the role of services. Whatever industry you are in, we are seeing physical goods and products, turn into services, which is fueled by KPIs, Big Data, and the "internet of things." While it has become easier to sell products to different markets than ever before, it does require customization in order to enter specific geographic markets. An understanding of the culture in a particular region and building relationships are essential to make the business a success. Academic research has shown a strong link between businesses having this global mind-set (Journals of International Entrepreneurship 2013). While we are embarking to going global, we should not forget the "PR power" of our local media.

CHAPTER 8

Local Media Love Small Businesses

When small business and organizations are embarking on their PR journey, I find that they tend to get swept up with the national media and forget their local media or perhaps do not value them as much, which is a shame. It is worth remembering that occasionally some of the big national headlines started as local news. Traditional local media outlets exist and should be integrated within a PR campaign.

These days' local media consist of not just the traditional media outlets such as newspapers, radio, television, but also local community groups, local newsletters, community magazines, networks, podcasts, and online platforms. They are all looking for strong news stories and can be very supportive of local companies and initiatives.

Local Media

Working with your local press is also a good way to communicate with your potential local customers and getting to know your local media is the way to go about it—*create a relationship*. There are so many types of local media ranging from local newspapers, community magazines, local newsletters, online community platforms, local radio, TV, and podcasts—and they all usually look for things that fit their news agenda and to interest their target audience. Some things to think about when approaching:

- *"News peg" your news story to pictures.* Your business on its own may not stand out, but maybe your personal story will be of interest—did you overcome adversity in some way to get going, or did you make a radical career change that people might find fascinating—city trader to sheep farmer, perhaps?

Or do you have views about local or industry issues that other people in your area or sector would find interesting and relevant? Think as creatively as possible to create a "news angle."

- *Look at the kind of stories the local media have featured in the past and find out their deadlines.* The local newspaper is usually weekly and therefore will have a what they call their "press day in the week," where they are frantically ensuring that they are filing all their copy deadlines. You need to find out in advance what is their press day, so you are not calling on this busy day and, of course, to ensure you are not missing the weekly deadline. It is important to give journalists as much notice as possible so they can plan when and how to cover your story.

- *Local Radio, TV, or Podcasts*—If you are speaking or being interviewed on radio or TV, prepare yourself for an interview. Check if the interview is live or pre-recorded. Also, if it is TV, will you be going into the studio or will they be coming to you? If they are coming to you, have your branding in the background of where the shot will be made.

  1. Find out how long the interview will be and what type of questions they will be asking, what their angle will be, so you can then prepare your responses. Prepare your key messages that you want to get across in the interview, having not more than four is ideal. Anything too complex or long will be difficult to get across.

  2. Speak clearly; slowly breathe. We tend to speak fast when nervous. Look at the interviewer, rather than the camera, and let your passion shine through.

  3. Find out what local business networks exist locally and get in touch with them, offering to give a talk at their next members meeting about the value your local business adds to the local business community, and offer their members a special discount. Find how you can add value to these local networks.

Tips When Dealing with Local Media

The more you understand how the journalist thinks, the more likely you are to be able to deliver something they are looking for; the bottom line is that they want something that will catch the attention of their readers, viewers, or listeners. The more you work with local press, the more they will remember you and come to you for comment on local issues relevant to your organization. Other things to consider:

Be Responsive

Reporters and editors are busy people; so if they call up looking for comment or opinion, get back to them as soon as possible. Reporters know people are sometimes hard to get hold of, so they will often put out a couple of calls—the company that responds most quickly gets the quote.

Waffling and Jargon

This is particularly important, if you are doing radio or TV, as your messages will get lost. Preparing your key messages in advance helps. Do not make the mistake of assuming everyone knows as much about your industry as you do. Do not speak in acronyms, as people will lose interest and have no idea what you are talking about. Try not to be too technical in language—speak in layman's terms—so anyone can follow your story.

Follow your local media on social media; so when your story comes out you can tag them into your social media post. Your social media post will gain more traction and reach.

Case Stories

A small local soccer academy in North London, called Turnstyles Football Academy, ran an international soccer camp with boys from Italy one summer. The Italian boys were on an exchange to play the game and improve their English. This was a great local story and we contacted the local newspaper, who came to interview soccer coaches and the boys. The newspaper also took some photos to accompany the feature. We also contacted the local newspaper in the Italian town that the boys came from, who loved the story, too. The local Italian paper ran a story, using the photos from the local North London paper, ensuring to credit the photographer and the source of the photos.

Another good story was when a group of women in a rural Indian village started their own chocolate-making business while still working on their farms. Their local city newspaper loved this "good news" story and did a feature; this story then caught the national headlines and an international platform also ran the story.

An author had published first book and contacted his local press to inform that he was doing a book signing in the local bookshop. It was a great photo-story for the local paper, who covered the story and also went on local radio to talk about his book.

Local charities do really well with their local media, as they are making a difference to the local community. I have worked with countless charities all over the world, who have been supported well by their local press for the work they are doing.

Summary

It is worthwhile reminding ourselves as small businesses or organizations that the headlines on our national newspapers or on our national television news can often come from local media.

When reporting on local news, events, and business or product launches, local and regional media play an important part in promoting and sustaining communities and small businesses at a local level. Local traders, charities, organizations, and community groups rely on this exposure and support from their local media to communicate effectively with both new and existing audiences. When trying to raise your profile as a small business or entrepreneur, where you might not otherwise be heard in other national media outlets, the local media papers can bring about real, positive PR for you. The local media, such as newspapers, are a source of trusted and accurate information. Do not ignore developing these relationships; they can be rewarding.

Contacting the media, whether local or national, or if radio, or a magazine, newspaper, or television show, there is an art and format, which is called pitching. In Chapter 9, I reveal all and how to do it with success.

CHAPTER 9

Pitching to the Media

When I talk to the media, many of them roll their eyes at the thought of some of the approaches they have received from PR people trying to pitch a story on behalf of a client. It is so important to understand the best ways to communicate with journalists and how to tell your story. It is about understanding what makes the media tick and the principles are very similar to contacting your local media. Do not be intimidated by the prospect of calling a reporter; remember, at the end of the day, they are all people and it is about building relationships.

How to Pitch to Print Media

Pitching a story to the media is much like a sales pitch. In preparing for the pitch there are several things that you should take into consideration before deciding who, when, and how to make that pitch.

- *Do Your Research*—This is the first thing to do and probably the most important point of all. Understand the topic you want to talk about and do your research on it. Google is a great resource to see what is being said on the Internet. Your research will help you define your angle before you make contact with the media—I believe media relations comprise 95 percent preparation and 5 percent execution.
- *Identify the Relevant Journalist*—If you want to interest a journalist, then read through back issues to find what she or he may have written previously on the topic. Also, find out the byline of a journalist who writes on similar subjects to the one you are trying to promote. This really helps and is a big motivator to get a journalist interested in you/your story.

- *Pitching to Major Media Outlets*—They expect at least a unique angle, if not exclusivity. Be smart. Manage your story and your relationships.

- *Journalists Prefer E-mail Pitches*—An overwhelming number of media these days prefer to receive e-mail pitches. Some will only accept pitches by e-mail, because it is less intrusive than receiving countless phone calls. Through your pitch you are supplying a professionally packaged information product that helps the journalist to do his or her job.

- *Preparing Your Pitch*—Draft a one-page fact sheet about your business or organization that includes a brief background and important features. Come up with two or three different story ideas in mind, in case the first one is not of interest. Be willing to get additional information for the journalist.

- *Get Straight to the Point*—The media work to deadlines and pressure. Do not waste their time by starting with pleasantries such as "I hope you are well," or "How are you today." Use conversational, personalized writing, but be direct. Use your first two to three sentences to say what you are pitching and why. What is the key point or angle you want to make? Say it up front so the recipient does not have to waste time by reading through to the end of the e-mail.

- *Clear E-mail Subject Heading*—The subject line is the most important line in the whole e-mail. Make it short and snappy. At times the subject line of many e-mail pitches is too vague and gives no idea of the content. This is when many journalists will delete it before reading any further. Avoid using clichés in subject lines, headlines, or lead paragraphs. Avoid hype and exaggeration. Avoid using subject lines that look like spam—anything with repeated exclamation points, or all caps is not likely to get past spam filters. There is so much competition and clutter with e-mails these days that you need to grab attention immediately. Check your signature and ensure it clearly shows your name, organization/business name, and any other information to help the journalist contact you. This helps recipients locate your e-mail if they want to find it later.

- *What's News*—You can safely use "new" in subject lines, if it is a "new survey on" or "new treatment" or "new technology" or "new app" and so forth. Other suitable angles include timeliness of the item, the extent of human interest, how unusual it is, the impact, conflict, well-known person or expert involved, a solution to a problem, or saves money or a smarter way. It could be a story of "a new music group coming to town."
- *Establish a Connection*—Demonstrate that you are genuinely interested and share at least one authentic reason for working together. It will go a long way. Do not get pushy and, if the journalist is not interested, move on and try another news outlet.
- *Radio and Television Newsrooms*—Often coverage is heavily dictated by the nature of the medium. TV requires visuals and radio requires a strong spokesperson. The person to contact for TV and radio news and current affairs shows is the producer of each program or its news desk.
- *Timing Is Crucial*—Find out the working hours of reporters and their deadlines so you can ensure your contact and supply of material cater to their needs.

Case Stories

A UK business author also had a business trip planned for India and wanted to publicize the book in this region. I worked ahead and contacted business editor on the Indian national newspapers, giving them the opportunity to interview the author when he was in India, and gave them a strong Indian news angle. The *Times of India* interviewed the author and ran the interview in its paper.

It is just not businesses that seek publicity, but media brands also want those column inches. This example demonstrates this and when at The Economist Group, the whole organization had a re-brand, which also included the well-known *The Economist* magazine. The re-brand allowed us to talk about the Group and created an opportunity for the CEO at that time to talk about her vision for this very highly regarded media organization. I pitched this angle to the international media and the CEO did interviews with both European nationals and North American media, thus greatly enhancing media coverage internationally.

A political commentator saw that a topic was trending in the news and was a subject that he was an expert on. The political expert wanted to pitch his position on the subject, which was different to a lot of the media conversations in the news. This was a time-sensitive story and we needed to get the story out immediately, before it disappeared. I called the news desks on the print media to see if they would take a comment from the political commentator or, better still, publish an opinion piece from him based on the topic. A national newspaper did just that and published an opinion. The key thing to remember here is that we had the opinion piece ready and could turn things around instantly, to ensure that we not only met the newspaper's timescales, but also were time-sensitive to the actual news item.

Pitching to Magazines

Magazines are different from other types of media. Because of their lead times, as they plan much further in advance, think six to eight weeks ahead. For instance, a February issue might close in mid-November; the time to contact the editor with your pitch would be at least two months in advance, so in September. Their editorial teams also are different. Usually and inappropriately people tend to send pitches to the editor in chief, whereas in fact they would have a much higher chance of success if they approached the right person on the magazine. So, getting to know the magazine you want to approach is essential before you send a pitch. Other things to think about:

- Just like you would pitch to a newspaper, you need to prepare a pitch—this is a common thread throughout when pitching to the media. Double check that the topic you are pitching falls into what the magazine actually covers; do your research with the story that you are offering, ensuring that the story and angle is a fit, and it is even better if you are offering an exclusive. The most successful pitches will fit into the theme and offer an angle the magazine has not covered previously.
- Remember, your pitch is up against a flood of e-mails, so do not include more information than you need to; short and sweet is the answer. Customize your pitch, so it seems personal.

- Get the timing right, as magazines plan out their content and as they adhere to a print production schedule.
- There is a difference when it comes to pitching print magazines versus digital publications. At some media outlets, there is a completely different editorial team working on the digital content to the print magazine, while, at other media brands, there are editors who work on both print and digital. Again, this is why it is important to know who you are pitching and what they cover on a day-to-day basis.

Case Stories

A business consultant with a new book on leadership wanted to break into the US market and raise his profile at the same time. I researched the business leadership and training magazines in North America to pitch the business consultant, knowing that the story would be published ahead. In doing so I ensured that the pitch was not time-sensitive, but still relevant to the outlets. We also offered the magazines free books for their readership, giving away ten copies of the book to the first ten readers who sent in their details. This book offer strengthened the relationship with the editor.

The breast cancer charity I used to work for did a lot with women's magazines, particularly during Breast Cancer Awareness Month, which takes place globally around the world in October. All the editorial pitching and planning would take place as early as July to ensure that everything was ready in time for the October issue, which was published in September.

A small US-based sustainable chocolate brand wanted to gain some publicity in Europe, particularly in the United Kingdom. We researched the various sustainability magazines and pitched a story based around the ethos of the chocolate; several magazines carried the story.

Pitching to Radio

Radio is a great medium to promote your business and reach your target audience, as radio programs have a specific audience of listeners, which allows you to communicate directly to your customers, clients, or a niche group of people. Pitching to radio is a little different than pitching to TV or print media because the news cycle is quicker, as well as that they have other segments and the journalists have different roles. Here are some tips to help you pitch to radio:

- We already know that a story needs to be newsworthy and, to be featured in a radio interview, you need to have something newsworthy or interesting that can be discussed. Maybe you are an expert on a topic that is currently in the news or maybe your business is doing something really exciting a journalist would be interested in. Your topic must appeal to the program's target audience and fit in around the topics they usually discuss.
- Get to know the segments and do some research into the radio programs your target audience listens to and get to know more about it. Some radio stations have specific segments you can pitch to—such as a business or finance segment or a women's panel discussion. Most radio stations have breakfast, morning, afternoon, and drive-time shows. If your story is news related these segments are a good place to pitch to.
- You need to find out who the best person is to pitch your story to, to ensure that it will be considered. In most cases this will be the program producer rather than the host of the show, as they are involved in planning the show's content. If you do not have access to a media database, you can find out who to pitch to by calling the radio station's switchboard and asking for the name and contact details of a specific producer or doing an online search.
- Do not try to plug your company and, while this might sound counterintuitive, journalists are not there to help you promote your business—their job is to commission great content that will interest their audiences. Plus, advertising rules are so strict these days, and they are not allowed to run stories that appear to promote products or services.
- It is better to call the radio producer to pitch your story, rather than an e-mail because radio journalists work at a very fast

pace and your e-mail may become lost. As a SME, when you are pitching to a journalist you will need to explain why you would be a great person to interview and why your interview would be of interest to the program's listeners. Always prepare your phone pitch beforehand and write down what you are going to say. You have a better chance of success if you appear confident, knowledgeable, and get your point across quickly.

- Some shows are recorded, and it is worth checking to find out if the interview is live or pre-recorded.
- It is a good idea to follow up your phone call with an e-mail straight away to further explain your pitch and why it is relevant and interesting for their listeners. Some things to include in your pitch and follow-up e-mail are:
  1. Your credentials;
  2. The topics you can discuss during the interview;
  3. Why your topic is newsworthy or of interest to the target audience;
  4. Your availability for interviews; and
  5. Your contact details.
- Timing is everything. Never call a radio journalist during a live broadcast or while they are on air, unless it is a talkback segment that you want to participate in. Know what times the radio program airs and make your call before or after the broadcast ends if this is the case.
- Radio and TV producers, particularly on regional programs, are always looking for experts and "talking heads." So if you have specific expertise, do not be afraid to pick up the phone and introduce yourself. Again, timing is everything with radio, so call when you know there will be opportunities coming up. For instance, if you are a financial expert, it can be a good idea to call up a few days before a government spending review.

Case Stories

A western energy company entering the market in Ghana wanted to raise its profile in the region and one of the ways we did this was to search the various Ghanaian radio programs and find the suitable sessions focused on energy and business segments. I then searched to see what topics were trending in Ghana around energy and business issues. I then sat down with the client with my findings, to see how we could add to the conversation. From these conversations, I created a strong news angle, which I pitched to the radio stations. We were successful with three different radio interviews lined up.

A female entrepreneur from New York was in London and wanted to maximize her business trip. Before she flew, we discussed what she could talk about and I put these topics into news angles and pitched this business woman to London radio stations with a business female focus. The female entrepreneur did one radio chat show and a podcast interview for a business women news platform.

Times Educational Supplement wanted to raise the profile of the paper's first-ever campaign, for literacy for children in Afghanistan. This was a great story for radio as we had strong voices representing this campaign, including some children who had fled Afghanistan; both BBC World Service and BBC News covered the story interviewing the children.

Pitching to TV

Pitching to TV producers might just get your business or organization in the spotlight and the things to remember are:

- Images make the story in TV and, irrespective of whether it is the evening news, a morning show, or a current affairs program, if you want your business story to get on TV you need to put some thought into the visuals. There is no point in offering a media release on your great new product or survey results if there are no images to go with them. Make it easy for the producer to say yes by suggesting a few different visuals or video contact they could use in relation to the story you are pitching and creates more chance of success.
- Be topical or, in other words, *newsworthy*. If you are aiming at a news program, you will need a strong news angle. Even if you are pitching to a morning show or current affairs program, you will have the best success if you link your pitch to

something topical. If the producers can relate your idea to a current story in the media, it gives them more incentive to run with the idea.

- Real people stories and interviews make the story come alive, so if you have interesting client and customer case studies who are happy to be interviewed, put them forward in your pitch. Give the producer an insight on the person's background, involvement, and experience.
- Depending on what time they film you, some TV shows "drop" the interviews into a program or other programs that may fit the story, so check to see if your interview will be live or pre-recorded.
- A producer will usually just skim the first few sentences of the hundreds of e-mails they receive daily, so you want your pitch to stand out. Do not wait until the third paragraph to get to the point; be up front and to the point.
- Again, like radio, TV producers will be put off, if you are pushing a product, an event, or a business without a good hook. Your business takes a back seat to the actual story; it is the story that will get you TV coverage.

Case Stories

The following client story is not only a great visual story, but it also had a strong news angle, which meant it was perfect for TV, particularly as a news item. Three women were participating in the "Talisker Whisky Atlantic Challenge," rowing across the Atlantic with the focus to break the world record for both men *and* women, plus were also rowing for a charity to raise awareness about plastic pollution. This story had all the elements for a good pitch and the local BBC news station loved the story, particularly as they could film the team of women with their boat practicing their rowing on the River Thames. This made local London news.

During the 2018 Commonwealth Games, which were held on the Gold Coast in Australia, many of the small businesses and local traders pitched themselves to the international TV crews that were in town to show and talk about how they were celebrating the Games and the great business boost the Games were bringing. It was great international coverage for these small businesses.

The Future of Newsrooms

While it is important to know how to communicate with the media, I think when we are running our own businesses or trying to raise the profile of our organization, we need to be aware of what is shaping the future of news, so we can be aware of these changes and strengthen our approaches. Why? So we can include these elements in our PR strategies, communications, and pitches.

One of the key driving features is "diversity" and that is not just diversity in business and organizations, but within the news and newsrooms. The issue of gender equality has been a huge focus globally, where media companies for the first time have been forced to reveal pay gaps between men and women. It has been revealed that women are "dramatically under-represented in the news" with less than a quarter, that is 24 percent of news subjects or interviewees being female (The Global Media Monitoring Project Report 2015).

There have been conversations in the United States and in the United Kingdom about the negative way in which people of color are reflected in the media—again highlighting the need for greater newsroom diversity.

Reuters highlighted diversity and the impact it will have on journalists (Reuters Institute for The Study of Journalism and Oxford University Report 2019). Reuters showed that more journalists will follow the example of Bloomberg business reporter Ben Bartenstein, who found that only 13 percent of his interviewees were female, and set out to remedy this—achieving his 50 percent target by proactively seeking out new and more diverse sources.

His colleagues helped build up lists of high-profile women in finance while Bloomberg launched a "New Voices" initiative to give media training to women executives.

More newsrooms will start to monitor gender and ethnic diversity of content on websites by counting the names of interviewees or analyzing pictures. This awareness in turn will hopefully make editors more aware of their own biases.

The British newspaper, *The Financial Times* (FT), created a dashboard that monitors the reading habits of existing female subscribers to encourage editors to create more content that might appeal to women (Digital New Project 2019, p. 31). But deeper research on gender preferences has also led to new products such as the "Long Story Short" newsletter—five stories you should not miss—curated by a female FT journalist. One unexpected by-product was that this newsletter also proved a hit with disengaged male readers!

So, what could this mean for you as a business or organization? Well, simply to make your stories "diversity strong" and "authentically strong." Diversity is not a fad or a phase; it is a change in mind-set and thinking. Be ahead of the curve and build this thinking into your PR strategies and your brand.

Summary

I think one of the clear takeaways from this chapter is that a lot of research and preparation needs to go into a media pitch, irrespective of the type of media—radio, television, newspapers, or magazines. It is not just accuracy of facts regarding your news story that is important, but the research to find the right journalist contact, understand what they write/report on. It also important for businesses to know what is happening in their sectors, to become experts and thought-leaders. Also, in this day and age, there is no excuse for a small business not be "diversity strong." By being inclusive in your messaging, you automatically strengthen your brand and stand out with the media. But when things do not go according to plan, then you need to know how to deal with the negative publicity. Chapter 10 is focused on "crisis management."

CHAPTER 10

How to Handle Negative Press

Thinking that bad publicity will not happen to you is not an option, as social media has opened it up with instant communications, which means it has also changed the rules of crisis communication management. If you find yourself in the spotlight for the wrong reasons, take the opportunity to show your business in the best possible light under the circumstances. Communication is the key to managing a PR crisis.

Managing Bad Publicity

Complaints from customers, faulty products can all make online news, including any crisis affecting your industry that could give your business or organization a bad name by association. If your business or organization is being criticized online, you need to respond quickly, honestly, and decisively. Ensure everyone who complains gets a rapid and an appropriate response.

Say that you are sorry that the problem has happened. If you are at fault, do own up immediately and importantly apologize! Do not ignore the problem thinking it will go away. Never say "no comment" as this sends out the message that you are in the wrong and at the same time suggests that you feel no remorse or perhaps that you have something to hide.

One thing is for sure and that is good customer service has not gone out of business. Thank the customer for complaining. Put yourself in your customer's shoes. You will have more empathy with the customer, and you should find a solution more quickly. Start with the view that the customer has a valid point.

Find out all the facts first before responding. Allowing the customer give you all the information helps you fully understand the situation and, if they are emotional, it will give them time to calm down.

Correct and learn from the mistake, otherwise this could lead to more complaints about the same thing in the future, because you have not fixed the problem. Inform the complaining customer that they have helped you improve the business. You could create a SWOT analysis here to help you turn it around.

If you have a team, listen to them, as they are much closer to the customers than you are. Ask them for their feedback and views regularly. Make changes if possible and it makes business sense to do so. Make sure their complaints are handled, too, and occasionally disgruntled employees can generate bad press if they decide to be vocal. Make sure your staff understands the importance of customer service and embody your firm's positive brand values.

Put in place procedures for handling customer complaints, so that a small issue does not become a big problem. The *Journal of Business Research* (Yilmaz, Varnali, and Kasnakoglu 2016) shows that the customers who are happy with the way their complaint was handled are more likely to give word-of-mouth recommendations; and I have been that customer.

How to Plan

Planning and sound preparation can significantly reduce the chances of getting bad press. Staff training is essential—your employees are your brand ambassadors. No matter what their role, any member of staff has the power to enhance or ruin the reputation of your business. So, if you are dealing with a negative PR story, then consider the following:

- Again, you need to respond immediately and have a plan. Make sure a spokesperson is available to talk to the press and others about what went wrong and what is being done about it.
- Keep the media, customers, your staff, and suppliers informed. Ensure that employees do not talk to the press without permission and direct enquiries from journalists to the official spokesperson.
- Tell your side of the story by posting written statements. Another key element of dealing with negative PR successfully is devising a positive message about your company. After

getting bad publicity, you will need to produce positive PR, through strong positive stories. These could be community projects and charity initiatives. At the same time, do ensure that you are conducting business in an authentic way.

Case Stories

As you might imagine, there are many bad publicity stories. Some may seem small, but often these will morph into full-fledged crises. Several cases illuminate this:

When I was head of PR at the National Federation of Women's Institute (NFWI), a not-for-profit organization with 250,000 members, the UK prime minister (PM) at that time, Tony Blair, wanted to attend the NFWI's annual conference to speak to its members. The organization issued an invitation to the PM to speak at the event, which was held at Wembley Arena, London.

We held many briefings with the PM's office of what the agenda would be that day and what would be good topics for the PM to speak on. Yet, in an extraordinary error of political judgment none of the briefings were heeded; instead the event was used as a platform to reposition the Labour Party, as a party of traditional values in a changing world. The PM's speech went down like a lead balloon and Tony Blair was slow-handclapped off the stage. It was captured by the national political media, who had been invited by the PM's office to the event. It not only became a national news story that ran for days, but an international story.

At that time of the story unfolding, the PM's office wanted to know what the NFWI would be saying to the press; I told them there was only one statement that we would be giving and that was the truth. I issued a press statement from the NFWI's chairman at that time, Helen Carey, OBE, DL, that went to all staff, the NFWI's regional centers, and the media. The statement was uploaded on to the website. We also sent the regional office's instructions to refer all national media enquiries to head office.

The Chairman, Helen Carey, went on to do interviews with all the national press and, when Helen was not available, I stepped in as spokesperson. There was a tsunami of front-page headlines—such as the *Daily*

Mirror's "Hand bagged," the *Daily Mail*'s "WI Ladies who humiliated Blair," and *The Guardian*'s "Blair bombs at WI."

This story could have gone either way for the NFWI but, by giving an honest and accurate account of the incident, we actually increased our membership during this period. The final evaluation of all the media coverage showed that the NFWI had come well and there was no damage to the brand. The NFWI was suddenly invited on popular TV shows that it only had dreamed of being on, up until that point.

A week after the PM's slow-handclapping news incident, one of the UK's bestselling national newspapers, *The Sun*, ran a sensational front-page story saying the NFWI was racist. It ran an alleged story of a regional office accusing the members of being racist. I immediately refuted the story, showing that it was not accurate, by providing facts. I demanded that *The Sun* run a story about the NFWI, focused on the organization's diversity policies, and that it should be on page two of the paper and not lost within the paper itself, especially as it had been front-page news, which they did a day later.

A story broke on January 19, 2019, on social media of how *Vogue* (the United States) misidentified Noor Tagouri, a journalist and an activist, as Noor Bukhari, who is a Pakistani actress and model, in its February 2019 issue. BBC News Online (https://www.bbc.co.uk/news/world-us-canada-46926747) was one of the many sources that reported this story, which went viral on social media, when Tagouri posted a video of herself capturing her excitement of seeing herself in the magazine, only then to immediately discover they had got her name wrong. *Vogue* made no excuses, and immediately owned up to its mistake and issued an apology. It quelled the story.

Remember the Doritos disaster? In an interview, Indra Nooyi, PepsiCo CEO, said gender differences were driving product development of its Doritos and said in an interview, "Women don't like to crunch too loudly in public and they don't lick their fingers generously, and they don't like to pour the little broken pieces and the flavor into their mouth" (Freakonomics 2018; Episode 316). Doritos scotched the talk of different chips, but not without a hearty round of jeering on Twitter. Model Chrissy Teigen, Glee star Jane Lynch, comedian Kathy Griffin, and actress Busy Philipps were among the many critics who took to social media to slam the idea. PepsiCo released a statement at the time, calling reporting on the launch of such a product "inaccurate," adding "we already have Doritos for women—they're called Doritos." Commentators on the story said at that time that Nooyi was a seasoned and high-profile food industry veteran, who knew what she was doing and was "trying to tap into the market." There's a view, which I share, that the more you talk about a brand and its product, the more sales go up and people are reminded the product still exists.

The British Petroleum (BP) Oil crisis that occurred in 2010 is a classic example of bad reputation management. The incident was the biggest offshore oil spill in the US history and was a tragedy and environmental disaster, exacerbated by the way the crisis was handled.

BP's lack of apparent empathy and compassion was personified by former BP CEO, Tony Hayward, who infamously said to a television crew filming for the *Today Show* (www.todayshow.com), "I'd like my life back," evoking a huge backlash of public resentment and anger. This was not the only PR mistake BP made during this crisis, as not only did their website have scant information on this situation, but there were also minimal links to Facebook and Twitter.

What should have happened is for Hayward to have been mindful of all his global operations and issued a strong message of empathy regarding the need for due diligence in safety.

There were not enough images of a hardworking CEO, in oil-stained work gear, directing crews like General working to make things better.

Sadly, the company was not at the front and center of the media. To minimize the damage, BP should have immediately set about doing four easy things:

1. Issued regular, frequent progress reports;
2. Controlled and updated the pictures regularly;
3. Been completely transparent about the incident; and
4. Displayed empathy.

Admittedly, BP has taken positive steps in recent years.

Whatever, PR crisis you are going through, the key is to face it head on, be empathetic, communicate regularly, and find the solution to make things better and improve.

Summary

Big or small, for profit or not-for-profit, all organizations should have a plan in place to manage any adverse situations, to protect the profitability, brand, and reputation of your organization. So many businesses do not have a crisis plan in place before a crisis occurs, which can lead them to be caught off guard when things go wrong and incorrect information goes viral in a matter of minutes. We can see from this chapter that developing a plan is not difficult; it just requires some thought to think of what types of situations could threaten your business and come up with a plan of how you would respond. If you wait until you are in an emergency situation, you will feel rushed and react emotionally. Importantly, remember no response is a response.

We know it is key to measure your PR efforts and, while I have discussed KPIs in Chapter 6, Chapter 11 really digs deep into measurement.

CHAPTER 11

Measurement

The efforts of PR can be wasted, if the outcome is not measured effectively and when you are a small business, charity, or organization you want to ensure that you are getting value for money and not wasting your time. If you are not measuring content and its success, how can you really tell the impact that your PR plan is having? This question has plagued PR for years, partially the fault of PR practitioners for not demonstrating that their efforts actually changed *behaviors* in the way intended (Michaelson and Stacks 2017).

The Research, Measurement, and Evaluation Conundrum[1]

Until recently only elementary and basic research was conducted on the effect of PR campaigns. Press clippings, for instance, let you know that the information was presented in some media, but not that anyone was impacted by it—that they were now aware of the issue, problem, or product—how and what they felt about those topics after being presented a message through the media—whether it added to their the knowledge to make a decision to act in the way intended—whether or not they would advocate for the issue, problem solution, or product (a major outcome of PR is what has been called the "third-person effect" whereby others than the clients or business express to their own circle of friends something, hopefully positive, about it—and, finally, behave as the campaign was designed to do (Stacks 2017).

Understanding that PR attempts to establish an expectation for behavior is important when deciding how to collect the data to measure

---

[1] An excellent addition to your PR library is Stacks and Bowen's (2013) *Dictionary of Public Relations Measurement, and Research,* 3rd ed., which is available for free from https://instituteforpr.org/dictionary-public-relations-measurement-research-third-edition/

Communication objectives

- **BASIC** communication objectives for public relations efforts:

    - ○ Build awareness

    - ○ Advance knowledge

    - ○ Sustain relevance

    - ○ Initiate action

    - ○ Create advocacy

Figure 11.1 The basic model and communication objectives

and evaluate a PR effort, whether a single event or a long-term campaign. Michaelson and Stacks (2017) suggest that PR should measure five basic outcomes in any campaign (see Figure 11.1). They call this outcome model B.A.S.I.C—measuring whether the campaign has built awareness, advanced knowledge, sustained relevance, initiated action, and actually created advocacy as planned. These are tied to the PR campaign's three primary objectives: (1) informational—get the information out to build awareness and advance knowledge; (2) motivational—sustain relevance of newly created attitudes and beliefs and lead the audience to initiate action; and (3) behavioral—both advocate for the campaign and then actually do what the campaign asked them to do.

What this does is establish behavioral outcomes that can be correlated to parts of your campaign to demonstrate effectiveness (and to provide benchmarks against which test to ensure your campaign is on phase and on target). Michaelson and Stacks (2017) call this "end-to-end" PR and creates a return on expectations (ROE) model that can predict return on PR investment (ROI). Li and Stacks (2015) demonstrated, for instance, that investment in social media (see Chapter 6) can be demonstrated to impact on business (financial) outcomes.

Collecting Data

Data collected to measure outcomes takes many forms. It may be simply measuring column inches or TV airtime or social media KPIs (key performance indicators). It may be more sophisticated and include content analysis of others' pickup of your messages and forwarding them to their followers and readers (i.e., a third-person effect). It may involve bringing together focus groups to better understand how your messages are being received. Or, it may involve survey research where random samples from audiences, publics, and stakeholder groups are queried regarding the campaign. While the first method is inexpensive, the other more sophisticated methods can become very expensive.

Triple A's

As noted, measuring PR can also help see what content was interesting and relevant, helping to guide future PR initiatives and campaigns. To be able to measure your PR success, there are three key factors I consider important, and I call them "Triple A's" and are:

1. *Audience*—Who do you want to reach? As specific as stakeholders or more generally as audiences, or, even larger, publics?
2. *Awareness*—What is your message? What do you want to achieve?
3. *Action*—What do you want the target audience to do after communications?

Once the aforementioned has been defined, you will know what you want to measure. But how do we, actually, quantify success? How do we actually measure the value of PR?

Well, years ago, irrespective where you were based (and is something my own teams have done in the past, to measure the PR value/success of a campaign), PR professionals would sit with a ruler and a bundle of newspapers, measuring the size and space of a piece of coverage. Yes, imagine that?! We would then use that information to measure something called the advertising, value equivalent (AVE) of that space. It was a long tedious job.

Yet, while the measurement of PR value has moved on since the days of literal interpretation of "column inches," the use of AVE still remains commonplace for many people who want an inexpensive way to indicate "success."

Advertising, Value Equivalent (AVE)

AVE refers to the cost of buying the space taken up by a particular article, had the article been an advertisement. AVE figures are still popular in some parts of the industry, because it is an easy way to show how much value you can get from PR. It is argued that AVE is a way to explain the value of PR to people who may not be familiar with marketing and media, when justifying investment in PR activity.

It refers to the number of people exposed to the coverage and whether people have had repeated exposure. It is considered an important qualifying measure, where the effectiveness of a campaign is dependent on the number of times a person sees it.

Yet, there has always been a big debate around the real value and meaning of AVE, which has raged on for years. However, even prior to the global recession in 2008, along with the beginnings of social media at the same time that greatly impacted the print media, advertising fell and, consequently, affected AVE. The European AMEC (https://amecorg.com/amecframework/) and the US Institute for Public Relations (https://instituteforpr.org/ipr-measurement-commission/) joined forces and issued in what is called the "Barcelona Principles" (https://instituteforpr.org/barcelona-principles-2-0-updated-2015/), a call for discontinuance of AVE as a *valid* measure of PR success. However, neither organization has offered a replacement metric of success.

How We Measure PR Today

Thankfully, PR measurement has evolved (no more sitting around with rulers!) and now the way we report about the success of PR efforts has changed significantly. It has become more important to measure the effects of PR, what target audiences now think, say, and do after exposure to PR, than it is to provide a financial mark of activity. Evaluation is now about message drive, delivery, and gaining a positive behavioral response. From media impressions to key message placement, there are a number of ways to measure the success of PR campaigns depending on your aims and objectives.

These are smarter, cost-effective, and fruitful ways to track and measure the success of a PR campaign. With the advent of social media, it is now possible to track your success. Here are some tools.

Using Social Media

We now know that social media has become an integral part of all PR campaigns and important part of engagement, helping you understand the tone and reach of your posts. Most communication campaigns focus on creating content that people want to talk about and share on social channels, increasing the importance of measuring the impact of social media.

Social media measurement tools have evolved extensively and there are many ways it can be measured; and all the social media platforms—LinkedIn, Facebook Page, Twitter, YouTube®, and Instagram—have their own free analytics, which shows you the engagement, reach, and tone of your posts.

While there is still value in measuring awareness of and engagement with your brand through the number of likes, comments, retweets, replies, and shares, the real payoff is measuring how these likes and shares turn into sales. Traffic driven to your site can be measured through tracking URL shares, clicks, and conversions; share of voice can be measured by tracking activity compared to that of competitors, so you can understand where your business/brand falls in the hierarchy.

Case Studies

For a global small "health therapy" business, we have been able to determine how different messages and channels of communication are affecting their reputation. We found what types of facts and information are important to drive influencers to speak and create conversations about them.

While working for a book publishing house, we determined if social media was driving sales. As it turned out there was no direct effect on sales, but Twitter was driving website visits and in turn these website visits drove sales.

At a leading breast cancer charity, we were able to isolate the impact of volunteer fundraising from various channels such as radio advertising and direct mailings. We found that we could raise more money for breast cancer research, if we began to shift more money toward online earned media.

As noted earlier, use of Facebook, Twitter, and YouTube® has been demonstrated to impact on corporate bottom line, both financially and socially (Li and Stacks 2015).

Website Traffic and Google Analytics

Website traffic provides an excellent way to see how well a PR campaign did, as measuring web traffic before (establishing a baseline) and after a campaign launch can help determine the PR campaign's success against baseline and benchmarks. Many businesses use website traffic and page views as a way to measure their success/impact.

Straightforward visitor numbers tell part of the story, but you should also drill down into web traffic by evaluating demographics including age group, location, and device (e.g., laptop, mobile phone, and tablet) to ensure you are reaching your target audience or specific stakeholder group. It is also important to measure where website traffic originates from to establish which sites and social media networks send the most traffic and create the most value for your brand.

A rise in new unique visitors indicates that brand awareness has grown, but it is also important to monitor returning visitor numbers—a good indication that brand trust has developed.

Engaging content, such as blog posts, infographics, and videos, encourages return visits and ensures your audience relies on your brand for inspiration or the latest information.

Another important web metric is "goal conversions" and this is whether their associated objectives are subscriptions, form completions, or e-commerce transactions; conversions enable you to track value of PR; if the PR campaign reaches the right target audience, it should increase the number of conversions or qualified leads.

Google Analytics

As discussed in Chapter 6, Google Analytics can help businesses and other organizations evaluate their PR efforts, giving a much more holistic overview about target audiences. The platform is arguably one of the most powerful tools to learn about your digital efforts and gain a better understanding of how PR is working with other marketing initiatives to achieve your objectives. It expands your measurement capabilities, offering additional insights into audience needs and online behaviors. Armed with these insights, you will be able to test new campaigns and tactics, and fine-tune for success. Here are some Google Analytics tips for tracking KPI activity and understanding your target audiences' behaviors:

Annotations—Google Analytics has a feature that allows you to insert annotations, or notes, for specific events. Use this feature to note the dates of when you send media releases, land a big piece of earned coverage, post a blog, launch a social campaign, or distribute an e-mail newsletter. Ideally, you will be able to correlate spikes in website traffic to a specific activity, or set of activities, taking place in the same timeframe. This can be a helpful metric to not only see how all of your marketing efforts are working together, but also whether or not the combined efforts are successful.

Referral Traffic—Looking at referral traffic can be useful to determine which outlets are driving traffic from earned coverage. This metric also provides insight into which social media platforms are successfully sending audiences to your website for additional information, which can help refine your content strategy. Having diverse traffic sources improves search engine optimization (SEO). Keep an eye on organic and search traffic to ensure you have a good mix of sources. This will help protect your site's overall performance should a search engine algorithm change.

New and Returning Visitors—It is important to understand if you are speaking to an existing audience or reaching a new audience. For example, a high percentage of returning visitors could be ideal for a regular blog post, as it indicates that the content is resonating with your readers, encouraging them to come back frequently for the latest posts. Whereas a lead-driven business would benefit from a high percentage of new visitors. Understanding this metric can help you determine how your content is performing and if a new direction is needed.

The Bigger Picture—Look at clicks and a user's digital footprint to see where they go after reading a blog post or press release. If someone is only on the site for a few seconds and clicked on eight different articles, it could be a sign they are not finding what they need, and it is time for a content strategy rethink.

Looking at multiple metrics helps tell a more comprehensive story about your users and what they need or want from your digital efforts.

Backlinks—Backlinks are among the most important factors in achieving high search engine ranking and boost your SEO, which increases web traffic. Gaining better search engine placement is a key measure of successful PR activity.

Google assigns greater value to legitimate backlinks from authoritative sources and your PR efforts can be critical in obtaining those backlinks through innovative and engaging content. The number of backlinks is a good metric for understanding if your audience finds your content relevant, useful, and valuable. After all, it is every business/brand's goal to appear on page one of Google!

Keywords

Keyword rankings can be used to measure specific terms you are trying to rank for and, if you do not rank for your most relevant keywords, your organic website traffic will decrease. This will affect lead generation and ultimately sales and revenue. Measuring keyword rankings enables you to ensure you're targeting the right keywords and to determine if your brand's page rank is improving over time. As you gain more backlinks, your site becomes more trusted.

Do-It-Yourself Media Monitoring

Another way to measure campaigns is to physically count the number of articles your organization's name appears and is the simplest measure for quantifying the success of a PR campaign. You can pay for this service, but if on a budget you can do this yourself manually.

Knowing the number of stories (or hits) your company generates and how those numbers stack up against the competition offers an insight of how your business is viewed by the media you are targeting. This do-it-yourself method has its advantages in terms of cost and connection to the news (all good PR people should monitor their media space). However, this method is extremely time-consuming and usually not comprehensive enough.

A step up from physically clipping articles is using online tools to create alerts for specific keywords, such as your company or product's name. Google, Yahoo!, and many news sites use something known as Rich Site Summary or commonly referred to as RSS feeds, and offer these services for free. Most deliver clips from at least a few sources, although they vary in selectivity, sensitivity, and range.

Web alerts are likely to grab articles that are not always pertinent, so you need to review each clip for relevance.

Clipping Services

Clipping services provide the best means for accurately and efficiently tracking coverage and is a paid for service, which can be costly. However, for a company intent on monitoring news coverage and determining their PR efforts, the expense is justified. Before the advent of the Internet, clipping services were staffed by individuals who would read, clip, and mail each individual article to their client; and over the years I have subscribed for this service when working for large organizations. When you received the articles, you would then have to manually catalog each piece of news.

These services are still available today, but the cost and unwieldiness make this option unattractive to most business owners. However, electronic clipping services provide a balance between accuracy, efficiency, and timeliness. Such services offer companies the ability to track a huge variety of media, including print, TV, and online sources. The best clipping services can scan tens of thousands of media outlets within a short time period and then deliver reports to your inbox on a continuous basis or as daily reports.

Electronic clipping services can be programmed to monitor a multitude of company names, keywords, and phrases. This gives you the opportunity to have them track not only your own coverage, but also that of your competitors and your industry. This kind of industry awareness can help you react quickly to unusual events and potentially alter your communication strategy as a result. Some clipping services will prioritize coverage based on publication type, readership, and geographic region. This additional data can be quite useful in assessing the impact of your coverage.

Market Surveys

One impartial way to demonstrate a change in perception could be an online poll of 1,000 people. Depending on your PR campaign, surveys can be used prior to the launch of your PR campaign to understand the current awareness and perceptions of the brand. Awareness statistics that trend upward will certainly prove the value of PR activity. However, commissioning and analyzing this kind of research can be expensive.

Trade Shows and Speaking Event Measurement

Sometimes, your PR activity might be staging trade shows, holding special events, meetings, and involvement in speakers' programs. For shows and events, obviously one possible output measure is an assessment of total attendance, not just an actual count of those who showed up, but an assessment of the types of individuals present, the number of interviews that were generated, and conducted in connection with the event, and the number of promotional materials that were distributed.

Summary

Ultimately, measuring the effectiveness of PR activity stems from having solid PR objectives from which success can be measured. To have the greatest impact on business results, PR must be measured to determine where it can be improved, and what its return on efforts, time, and investment really is. Each of the metrics mentioned in this chapter will not give a full picture of how successful a PR campaign has been on their own, but when combined and cited against your business objectives you will clearly see the effectiveness of your PR activity.

CHAPTER 12

The Power of Serendipity in Business

What Is Serendipity

Over the course of my career in PR, I have learnt about the power of serendipity in business and it is something that I like to talk about with small businesses and the self-employed. Essentially, it is associated with how we network and the importance of networking, which is all part and parcel of PR—remember Chapter 1 in this book—*PR is all about relationships and people.*

Being connected both online and off-line is a strong tool for small, medium-sized businesses (SMEs) because it creates opportunities and, when we build a solid network of global contacts, we are also creating potential business for ourselves.

Serendipity itself means "fortunate happenstance" or "pleasant surprise" and was coined by English art historian Horace Walpole in 1754 suggested by *The Three Princes of Serendip*, a fairy tale, where the heroes "were always making discoveries, by accidents and sagacity, of things they were not in quest of" (Interesting Literature, "A Short History Of The Word Serendipity" https://interestingliterature.com/2015/01/28/a-short-history-of-the-word-serendipity/).

Perhaps the most famous example of serendipity is the accidental discovery of penicillin, a group of antibiotics used to combat bacterial infections. In 1928, Scottish biologist Alexander Fleming took a break from his lab work investigating staphylococci and went on holiday. When he returned, he found that one Petri dish had been left open and a blue-green mold had formed. This fungus had killed off all surrounding bacteria in the culture. The mold contained a powerful antibiotic, penicillin, that could kill harmful bacteria without having a toxic effect on the human body. Fleming's chance discovery has been credited as the moment when modern medicine was born.

Characteristics of Serendipity

The first thing to learn is that *serendipity is unpredictable and that it happens more when you work hard*, but is not always there because you tried hard.

While you cannot predict when it happens, you can sometimes have a good guess. Luck and serendipity are often connected, and I, too, have mistakenly thought in the past that these two are linked, but I have learnt through experience that these two terms are actually quite different; because to become a wizard of serendipity you need to navigate and strategize until you are positioned in the right place at the right time, while to be lucky is to simply find oneself in the right place at the right time. There is a subtle, important difference.

The more we plan our PR and work online and off-line, we can create serendipity for ourselves. When we create a place where everyone who is connected to a business can interact, you automatically create a place where chance encounters are happening at every minute. Serendipity is an approach that should be cultivated and practiced at all times. It is not an abstract concept. It happens best when we are networking and using social media—we increase our chances of it happening. The more we work at what we do then the better are our chances for serendipity to occur. "Serendipitous networking" requires awareness, patience, and perseverance; as new relationships arise, these connections mature, and evolve. As a business owner and entrepreneur, you can easily see how serendipity networking gives you a better return on investment (ROI) on your relations capital.

It is a significant factor in both the creative process and the business process and *Harvard Business Review's* CEOs revealed one pattern, which is the most successful leaders and their companies have increasingly, and usually subconsciously, been developing a muscle for serendipity (Global CEO Study 2017-2018).

The Four Principles

There are some things we can do to increase and build serendipity in our lives, which I believe thrives on four principles:

1. *Be random, open, and flexible.* We are conditioned not to talk to strangers, yet some people enter our lives and change them forever. Do not just aim to talk to the people you think you need to when at events, because you just do not know who the other people in the room are connected to and who they may know?! Do not keep networking in the same pool, go out and be flexible. Accept invitations to connect from people outside your sector, as you do not know who they know and what opportunities might be waiting for you. What we do know is that when you are more serendipitous in your outlook, we create opportunities and possibilities—which is always good for business.

2. *Be helpful.* Go out of your way to be kind, friendly, and helpful to everyone—they are likely to pay you back and remember you. I have found that "paying it forward" is one of the key principles of serendipity. There is always room for everyone. Plus, it is a fact that we always remember the kind, good people.

3. *Get out there.* You need to be active online and off-line—connecting with people. Conversations cannot happen if you are not visible or participating. Action is needed. There may be occasions when you keep seeing the same person at different events or when networking. Do not ignore the person, go and get to know them, introduce yourself, and explain that you have been at the same events recently and that you thought you would say hello. I have done this and made some great connections.

4. *Always be ready.* Most of your networking will not occur from Monday to Friday between 9 a.m. and 5 p.m.; unexpected conversations are the stuff serendipity networking is made of! Always have business cards on you.

Tony Hsieh, an American serial entrepreneur who co-founded Zappos, an online shoe and clothing retailer, who is also co-founder of the Downtown Project in Las Vegas, is a firm believer in serendipity. He has tried to cultivate serendipity at the Zappos headquarters, where the office has only one entrance, so employees from all departments run into each other. Hsieh has said, "Meet lots of different people without trying to extract value from them. You don't need to connect the dots right away. But if you think about each person as a new dot on your canvas, over time, you'll see the full picture" (Inc.com 2013).

Frans Johansson's 2015 book, *The Click Moment*, is about making that moment happen. He researched successful people and organizations, showing a common theme—a random moment occurs and they take advantage of it to change their fate—a "click moment" of unexpected opportunity. In his book he uses stories from history to illustrate the specific actions we can take to create more click moments, open ourselves up to chance encounters. I have included some stories here that sum up "serendipitous business moments," such as, when Diane von Furstenberg randomly saw Julie Nixon Eisenhower on TV wearing a matching skirt and top, which led Furstenberg to create the timeless, elegant wrap-dress. Today Furstenberg has shops in 65 countries. Johansson writes, "We can't escape the role randomness plays in our success or failure, but we can utilize its tremendous and enduring power" (p. 89).

Howard Schultz in his interview with the *Daily Telegraph* (2001) talks about creating relationships with people around the world, authentic experiences, and about doing something unplanned. These are all the elements of serendipity. In fact, in 1983, Schultz, then Director of Retail Operations and Marketing for Starbucks, went to Milan to attend an international housewares show. The Seattle company was not yet everywhere. Schultz took a break from the conference schedule to sample the local flavors, discovering that the Italian city's cafés were packed. Sipping a latte, he realized that people were not drinking coffee because of the equipment used, but because of communal experience—that was the business for Starbucks.

Case Stories

Setting yourself apart is one of the best bets for success and is what chef Marcus Samuelsson did when he bid to make a state dinner for President Obama in honor of visiting Indian Prime Minister Manmohan Singh. Johansson (2015) noted that knowing that the other 16 chefs in the running would be cooking within the bounds of White House tradition—French American cuisine had been served at every state dinner since 1874—the fusion-thinking Samuelsson decided to differentiate himself, suggesting a menu of Indian-American dishes, including veggies from Michelle's backyard garden. "The problem was that I was going head-to-head with

15 other excellent chefs. If we all proposed exceptional, but mostly traditional, menus it would be a crapshoot," he told Johansson, "They would either accept my separate approach or they wouldn't. If they liked it…I had no real competition. I would win." Samuelsson was selected. Johansson writes that "by rejecting the expected he opened himself up to a number of immediate insights that separated him from his competitors and greatly improved his odds for success" (p. 135).

Through my own "serendipity moments" I have connected to a wealth of expertise, business and personal contacts. I have also collected some pretty amazing business stories along the way.

A business woman in London noticed a new florist that had opened at her local tube station. At this time this particular lady was looking for a celebrity to support her charitable cause. She decided to go in and give some local support and bought some flowers. While there she started a conversation with the florist, discovering that this florist's biggest customer was Simon Cowell. The rest as they say is history.

Serendipity can cross continents and once while giving a talk about the "power of serendipity in business" at a local London business forum, during the Q&A session, someone stood up and said they wanted to connect me to their friend who is in Los Angeles (LA) and a songwriter. I was open to be connected and, two years later when I happened to be in LA for work, I met her friend, who in turn connected me to his friend, and his friend became one of my closest and long-standing clients—P.F. Sloan.

The PR strategy for P.F. Sloan was built on serendipity and this was a project with practically no budget. When I first met Sloan in LA in early June 2013, he had written his memoirs with his co-writer Steve Feinberg and they wanted a UK publishing house. When I came back to London that same month, I contacted four publishing houses and it was Jawbone Press who said they wanted to publish the book. They were looking for that last title that they felt was missing from their 2013 list. Everything was signed off by the end of that June, a rarity in publishing.

But the most significant serendipity story was I when had this deep gut feeling that I had to get P.F. Sloan to perform at Glastonbury in 2014 on the back of his London book launch and tour. I drew on my connections and had people connect me to the top dogs in the music business to help connect me to the organizers at Glastonbury, but nothing happened.

I could have given up, but I was convinced this was going to happen and, importantly, had to make it happen. I decided to e-mail Glastonbury myself and found a contact e-mail on its official website. Within three hours of sending that e-mail, one of the organizers at Glastonbury contacted me to say that they would love to have the legendary P.F. Sloan perform and that is what happened. P.F. Sloan went to Glastonbury the same year Dolly Parton was there.

Some of my clients have come from random connections on social media, including one small business based in Las Vegas, who was looking for a London-based PR agency. This was a great opportunity that also grew my network in Las Vegas itself.

I connected a local photographer that I knew to a global business leadership forum, who wanted a good photographer to take photos at their key events. A year later, this photographer is still working for this organization and recently saw a high-profile business woman at one of these events, a business woman she had heard of and who had influenced her own life. This photographer took her chance and went to introduce herself to this influential business woman. They swapped business cards. Now this local photographer is working for this very business woman! This story holds all the principles of serendipity—paying it forward, flexibility, grabbing an opportunity—to make this business opportunity happen.

I heard this great story about Bill Clinton when he was governor, who made it his duty to shake everyone's hand in the room—whether they were important or not. When asked why he went to so much trouble, Clinton replied, you just do not know who people are connected to.

"The Book Fairies" was a brilliant idea that launched in 2017 to inspire people to read books based on the principle of serendipity, which has now become a global business. The idea was simple and based on the premise that there are people around the world who like to read and share the books they have read. Combined with the fact that everyone loves a surprise, that is how "The Book Fairies" was created—giving people a chance to pop a sticker and some ribbon on a book, and leave it somewhere to be discovered! "The Book Fairies" can be anywhere and is for anyone—readers and authors; it is a clever business idea that not only helps to promote books but also authors. "The Book Fairies" has almost 9,000 people sharing books in over 100 countries!

In a world dominated by precision and efficiency, it is important to change the mind-set and perception of serendipity as loss of managerial control. Instead, see it as a sign of an open mind and a positive corporate culture that is crucial to avoid losing potentially serendipitous, valuable outcomes. Companies like Google are a great example of doing this and have learned to find a creative balance between their goals and a world that is completely unpredictable. As a small business, start-up, or being self-employed it means being out there, where people can find you. It means investing in creating your social media profiles on different platforms and being active. It also means being open to network with different people, which allows you to be connected to the connected.

Summary

Building relationships is part and parcel of good PR and in turn helps a business or organization to thrive and grow. The Internet and social media make it easier for us to create partnerships and collaborations. While off-line and real-time networking, being open to connect with others outside your sector can also be rewarding, bringing with it opportunities. The trick is not to put a time frame on when you think that these opportunities may come your way, because then you are automatically putting pressure on yourself and closing down your ability to be open. There is no science or algorithm to serendipity; it is based very much on trusting your instincts, which is good skill to have in business.

CHAPTER 13

Conclusion

The guiding principles of PR are creating connections by being an open networker, making time for your social media activity, developing a global mind-set, and using news and content to put forward a message about anything, whether a service, a product, a business, an organization, or a campaign. We now know that PR is *not* advertising, but is all about *relationships, punchy storytelling, image shaping,* and *engagement*; it is an ongoing influence that has been able to withstand the test of time. While the rise in digital media has shaken up traditional ideas of press coverage and in today's online world, PR is about making business social. While every SME and organization type is dependent on its reputation, PR strategy can be critical to the success of a small business. Strong PR planning, which integrates traditional media with new media, is making a real impact.

There is one thing that we can all agree on, and that is PR is not about "spin." There is no room for it. Instead it is very much a skill that involves empathy to develop and nurture *strategic* relationships with the media, your business collaborators, clients, and those within your network. The more personal you make your PR campaigns, the stronger the results will be, and the less chance of your campaign being replicated by someone else. At the heart of PR is *storytelling* and, when your story is driven by your passion and shaped by your experience, it will directly speak to your audience and that means success.

Humor and cleverness is one of the best ways to appeal to your audience, including supporting authentic causes such as diversity, sustainability, and climate change. The following are strong international examples:

- In 2013 the Procter and Gamble brand launched #LikeAGirl, which became a confidence movement, where the campaign was a huge success online and supported by a video from filmmaker Lauren Greenfield, which featured people of all ages interpreting the phrase "like a girl." The campaign team also worked with influencers and top media in tackling girls' low confidence during puberty. The United Nations acknowledged the impact the campaign had on female empowerment with an award.

- In 2010, American Express launched Small Business Saturday—a shopping holiday in the United States on the first Saturday after Thanksgiving. The idea was to encourage shoppers to shop locally, supporting small businesses, and is now a very popular initiative in the United Kingdom.

- On International Women's Day in 2018, McDonald's flipped its iconic golden arches upside down, turning the "M" into a "W" to honor women all around the world for their hard work, dedication, and accomplishments. The campaign reaped around 1.6 billion impressions and dominated Google as the No.1 brand query on International Women's Day. McDonald's Chief Diversity Officer Wendy Lewis said in a statement, "In celebration of women everywhere, and for the first time in our brand history, we flipped our iconic arches for International Women's Day in honor of the extraordinary accomplishments of women everywhere and especially in our restaurants" (Business Insider 2018).

While the quantity of coverage is important, *quality* of that coverage is even more so and you can work toward quality by staying relevant and ahead of the curve. It is crucial to constantly read, research stories and articles within your target market in order to note any new editors, writers, columnists and so forth, and then craft a thoughtful pitch to fit.

Remember, good PR takes time; it is about building blocks and putting the foundations in place. Therefore, you need to give it at least three to six months to see the benefits, which is not always in the form of instant sales. Just because your company is featured in the news, it does not mean you will instantly see a jump in sales. Essentially, PR builds credibility, trust, reputation, and brand recognition.

Keeping all this in mind, all that is left for me to say is thank you for choosing this book, *The PR Knowledge Book*, and good luck with your PR campaigns.

Enjoy creating your brand values. Have fun with it all, because when it stops being fun, it automatically becomes hard. Please feel free to connect with me on LinkedIn, Twitter, my Facebook Business Page, and Instagram.

References

2018 Global Digital reports from We Are Social and Hootsuite. 2019. https://datareportal.com/reports/digital-2019-global-digital-overview (accessed April 20, 2019).

Alternatives. 2019. https://alternatives.org.uk/ (accessed April 22, 2019).

Amec Integrated Evaluation framework. 2019. https://amecorg.com/amecframework/ (accessed April 20, 2019).

American Express Small Business Saturday. 2019. https://americanexpress.com/us/small-business/shop-small/about (accessed April 22, 2019).

Baidu. 2019. https://baidu.com/ (accessed April 22, 2019).

Bangladesh Caterers Association. 2019. http://bca1960.com/ (accessed April 22, 2019).

Barcelona Principles. 2019. https://instituteforpr.org/barcelona-principles-2-0-updated-2015/ (accessed April 20, 2019).

Bartenstein, B. 2019. https://benbartenstein.com/ (accessed April 22, 2019).

BBC News Online. 2019. Tagouri, N. https://bbc.co.uk/news/world-us-canada-46926747 (accessed April 20, 2019).

BBC News. 2019. https://bbc.co.uk/ (accessed April 21, 2019).

BBC World Service. 2019. https://bbc.com/aboutthebbc/whatwedo/worldservice (accessed April 21, 2019).

Bit.ly. 2019. https://bitly.com/ (accessed April 23, 2019).

Black Lives Matter. 2019. https://blacklivesmatter.com/ (accessed April 22, 2019).

Blair, T. 2019. https://institute.global/ (accessed April 22, 2019).

Bloomberg New Voices. 2019. https://bloomberg.com/company/announcements/newvoicesinitiative/ (accessed April 22, 2019).

Body Shop. 2019. https://thebodyshop.com/en-gb/about-us/our-heritage (accessed April 20, 2019).

Branson, R. 2019. On LinkedIn. https://linkedin.com/in/rbranson/ (accessed April 22, 2019).

Breast Cancer Awareness Month. 2019. https://who.int/cancer/events/breast_cancer_month/en/ (accessed April 22, 2019).

Britannica's website for the Epic of Gilgamesh. 2019. https://britannica.com/topic/Epic-of-Gilgamesh (accessed April 20, 2019).

Brogan, C. 2019. www.facebook.com/broganchris (accessed April 20, 2019).

Buffer. 2019. https://buffer.com/ (accessed April 23, 2019).

Business Insider. 2018. https://businessinsider.com/mcdonalds-flips-arches-upside-down-2018-3?r=UK (accessed April 20, 2019).

Business Insider. 2017. https://businessinsider.com/instagram-rolls-out-shoppable-posts-for-more-merchants-2017-10?utm_source=feedly&utm_medium=referral&r=US&IR=T (accessed April 20, 2019).

Buzzing Business Club. https://facebook.com/groups/buzzingbusiness/ (accessed April 22, 2019).

Cherry, M. 2019. https://issuu.com/charteredinstituteofpr/docs/11597_cipr_client_guide_v15?e=35763234/66164496 (accessed April 20, 2019).

Chopra, D. 2019. https://deepakchopra.com/ (accessed April 23, 2019).

CIPR's A guide to selecting PR agencies and independent practitioners. 2019. https://issuu.com/charteredinstituteofpr/docs/11597_cipr_client_guide_v15?e=35763234/66164496 (accessed April 20, 2019).

Coca Cola. 2019. https://www.coca-colacompany.com/our-company/mission-vision-values (accessed April 20, 2019).

Commonwealth Games 2018. 2018. https://gc2018.com/ (accessed April 22, 2019).

Consumer Electronic Show. 2019. https://ces.tech/ (accessed April 22, 2019).

Contartese, J. 2019. http://joelcontartese.wpengine.com/my-story/ (accessed April 20, 2019).

Daily Mirror. 2002. "Daily Mail." https://inews.co.uk/news/uk/tony-blair-slow-hand-clapped-by-the-womens-institute/ (accessed April 22, 2019).

Daily Telegraph. 2001. https://telegraph.co.uk/culture/4722384/The-buck-starts-here.html (accessed April 20, 2019).

Downtown Project. 2019. https://dtplv.com/ (accessed April 23, 2019).

Elfasi, H. On Instagram. @Elfasihayajewelry. 2019. (accessed April 21, 2019).

ESPN/Michael Jordan. 2013. http://espn.com/blog/playbook/dollars/post/_/id/2918/how-nike-landed-michael-jordan (accessed April 22, 2019).

Essar Foundation. 2019. https://essar.com/foundation/vision-and-approach/ (accessed April 22, 2019).

Essar Global Fund Ltd. 2019. https://essar.com/about/essar-global-fund-limited/ (accessed April 23, 2019).

Facebook. 2019. https://facebook.com/ (accessed April 22, 2019).

Facebook Business Page. 2019. https://facebook.com/business/pages/set-up (accessed April 22, 2019).

Fleming, A. 2019. https://nobelprize.org/prizes/medicine/1945/fleming/biographical/ (accessed April 22, 2019).

Forbes. 2017. https://forbes.com/sites/forbesagencycouncil/2017/02/03/video-marketing-the-future-of-content-marketing/#2cebfb546b53 (accessed April 22, 2019).

Forleo, M. On Twitter. 2019. @MarieForleo. (accessed April 21, 2019).

Freakonomics. 2018. Episode 316. http://freakonomics.com/podcast/indra-nooyi/ (accessed April 22, 2019).

Garst, K. 2019. www.facebook.com/kimgarstbiz/ (accessed April 22, 2019).

Gilbert, E. 2019. https://elizabethgilbert.com/ (accessed April 23, 2019).

Glastonbury. 2019. https://glastonburyfestivals.co.uk/ (accessed April 22, 2019).

Global CEO Study. (2017-2018). https://leadersonpurpose.com/the-ceo-study (accessed April 22, 2019).

globalwebindex. 2019. https://blog.globalwebindex.com/chart-of-the-day/twitter-now-the-fastest-growing-social-platform-in-the-world/ (accessed April 22, 2019).

Google Analytics. 2019. https://marketingplatform.google.com/about/analytics/ (accessed April 22, 2019).

Google Market Finder. 2019. https://thinkwithgoogle.com/tools/market-finder/ (accessed April 22, 2019).

Google Small Business. 2019. https://youtube.com/user/GoogleBusiness/ featured (accessed April 22, 2019).

Greenfield, L. 2019. https://youtube.com/watch?v=kCKPz3xn3sY (accessed April 22, 2019).

Griffin, K. 2019. On Twitter @KathyGriffin. https://twitter.com/kathygriffin (accessed April 22, 2019).

Halal Branding. 2018. Publisher Claritas Books. https://amazon.co.uk/Halal-Branding-Jonathan-J-Wilson/dp/1905837577 (accessed April 23, 2019).

Harvard Business Review. 2019. https://youtube.com/user/HarvardBusiness/ featured (accessed April 22, 2019).

Hello!. 2019. https://hellomagazine.com/ (accessed April 22, 2019).

Hootsuite. 2019. https://signuptoday.hootsuite.com/pro-uk-branded/?utm_source=google&utm_medium=cpc&utm_campaign=selfserve-bau-emea-en-ner-uk-pua-search-branded-exact&utm_term=hootsuite&gclid=CjwKCAjw7_rlBRBaEiwAc23rhtXdGYqVevCuoroubWJ1cC5XxCimp42TIsES7DwlqrKxk4l8RX4OuhoCKCEQAvD_BwE (accessed April 23, 2019).

Hsieh, T. 2019. https://facebook.com/tonyhsieh/ (accessed April 23, 2019).

Hubspot. 2019. https://blog.hubspot.com/marketing/video-marketing-statistics #sm.0000f7ujhkwrse8sqa62aq63w23fi (accessed April 22, 2019).

Inc.com. 2013. https://inc.com/magazine/201302/rules-for-success/rule-2-tony-hsieh-maximize-serendipity.html (accessed 22 April 2019).

Indian Zing. 2019. https://indian-zing.co.uk/hammersmith-restaurant-indian-zing-about/ (accessed April 22, 2019).

Instagram. 2019. https://instagram.com/ (accessed April 22, 2019).

Institute for Public Relations. "Measurement Commission." https://instituteforpr.org/ipr-measurement-commission/ (accessed April 22, 2019).

Interesting Literature. 2015. A short history of the word serendipity. https://interestingliterature.com/2015/01/28/a-short-history-of-the-word-serendipity/ (accessed April 22, 2019).

Jenner, K. 2019. Twitter @KendallJenner. https://twitter.com/KendallJenner?ref_src=twsrc%5Egoogle%7Ctwcamp%5Eserp%7Ctwgr%5Eauthor (accessed April 22, 2019).

Johansson, F. 2015. *The click moment*. Publisher Penguin Rando House. https://penguinrandomhouse.com/books/310450/the-click-moment-by-frans-johansson/9781591846833/ (accessed April 22, 2019).

Journal of Business Research. 2019. https://researchgate.net/publication/281781314_How_do_firms_benefit_from_customer_complaints (accessed April 22, 2019).

Journal of International Entrepreneurship. 2013. https://link.springer.com/article/10.1007/s10843-013-0105-1 (accessed April 22, 2019).

Kaneshka. 2019. https://kaminee.co.uk/product-category/resort-wear/resort-kaftans/ (accessed April 22, 2019).

Kattan, H. On Instagram. 2019. @hudabeauty (accessed April 21, 2019).

L'Oreal/Dame Helen Mirren. https://loreal-paris.co.uk/inside-loreal-paris/our-ambassadors/helen-mirren (accessed April 22, 2019).

Labour Party. 2019. https://labour.org.uk/ (accessed April 22, 2019).

Li, C., and D.W. Stacks. 2015. *Measuring the Impact of Social Media on Business Profit & Success: A Fortune 500 Perspective.* New York, NY: Peter Lang.

LID Publishing. 2019. https://lidpublishing.com/ (accessed April 22, 2019).

LinkedIn Official Blog on Terms of Service. 2019. https://blog.linkedin.com/2013/08/19/updates-to-linkedins-terms-of-service (accessed April 22, 2019).

Loving Local Enfield. 2019. https://facebook.com/groups/optician/ (accessed April 22, 2019).

Lynch, J. 2019. On Twitter @JaneMarieLynch. https://twitter.com/janemarielynch?ref_src=twsrc%5Egoogle%7Ctwcamp%5Eserp%7Ctwgr%5Eauthor (accessed April 22, 2019).

Marketing Week. 2016. https://marketingweek.com/2016/02/28/why-brand-storytelling-should-be-the-foundation-of-a-growth-strategy/ (accessed April 22, 2019).

Michaelson, D., and D.W. Stacks. 2017. *A Professional and Practitioner's Guide to Public Relations Research, Measurement, and Evaluation.* New York, NY: Business Expert Press.

Mobile Marketing Association Asia. 2019. www.mmaglobal.com/research (accessed April 22, 2019).

Muck Rack and Zeno Group. 2018. https://muckrack.com/blog/2018/05/22/2018-muck-rack-survey-results (accessed April 22, 2019).

National Federation of Women's Institutes. 2019. https://thewi.org.uk/ (accessed April 22, 2019).

Nike/Lance Armstrong. 2019. https://news.nike.com/lance-armstrong (accessed April 22, 2019).

Ok!. 2019. https://ok.co.uk/ (accessed April 22, 2019).

Pepsico. 2019. https://pepsico.com/brands/product-information (accessed April 22, 2019).

Pew Research. 2018. https://journalism.org/2018/09/10/news-use-across-social-media-platforms-2018/ (accessed April 22, 2019).

Pew Research. Millennials. 2019. https://pewresearch.org/topics/millennials/ (accessed April 22, 2019).

Pink Ribbon Ball. 2019. https://breastcancernow.org/get-involved/fundraise-for-us/special-events/pink-ribbon-ball-london (accessed April 22, 2019).

Podcasts Insights.com. 2019. www.podcastinsights.com/podcast-statistics/ (accessed April 22, 2019).

Podium. 2017. http://learn.podium.com/rs/841-BRM-380/images/2017-SOOR-Infographic.jpg (accessed April 22, 2019).

Polaroid/Lady Gaga. https://polaroid.com/news/lady-gaga-named-creative-director-for-specialty-line-of-polaroid-imaging-products (accessed April 22, 2019).

Power, T. 2019. On Twitter. @ThomasPower (accessed April 21, 2019).

Procter and Gamble. 2019. #LikeAGirl. https://news.pg.com/blog/LAGkeep playing (accessed April 22, 2019).

Qualman E. 2019. https://equalman.com/ (accessed April 22, 2019).

Research and Markets. 2018. https://prnewswire.com/news-releases/video-streaming-market-worth-usd-7005-billion-by-2021---online-video-streaming-has-increased-viewership-60---research-and-markets-300267717.html (accessed April 22, 2019).

Reuters Institute for The Study of Journalism and Oxford University Report. 2019. https://agency.reuters.com/content/dam/openweb/documents/pdf/news-agency/report/journalism-media-and-technology-trends-and-predictions-2019.pdf (accessed April 22, 2019).

RFI Group. 2018. U.K. https://rfigroup.com/rfi-group/news/uk-press-release-amazon-and-paypal-more-trusted-among-younger-generation-banks-hold-their (accessed April 22, 2019).

Rodriguez-Nieto, A. 2019. https://antonionietorodriguez.com/ (accessed April 22, 2019).

Roth, D. Editor-In-Chief, LinkedIn. 2018. https://linkedin.com/pulse/linkedin-top-voices-2018-influencers-daniel-roth/ (accessed April 22, 2019).

Rule, J. 2019. on Twitter. @Ruleyork

Siang, S. 2019. On LinkedIn. https://linkedin.com/in/sanyin/ (accessed April 22, 2019).

Sloan, P.F. 2019. https://imdb.com/name/nm0806000/bio (accessed April 22, 2019).

SmartInsights 2019. www.smartinsights.com/social-media-marketing/social-media-strategy/new-global-social-media-research/ (accessed April 22, 2019).

Smith, M. 2019. www.facebook.com/marismith/ (accessed April 22, 2019).

Socialnomics. 2019. https://socialnomics.net/about-us/ (accessed April 22, 2019).

Stacks, D.W. 2017. *Primer of public relations research,* 3rd ed. New York: Guilford Press.

Stacks, D.W., and S.A. Bowen. 2015. *Dictionary of Public Relations Research and Measurement,* 3rd ed. Gainesville, FL. https://instituteforpr.org/dictionary-public-relations-measurement-research-third-edition/ (accessed April 22, 2019).

Stanford Graduate Business School. 2019. https://youtube.com/channel/UCGwuxdEeCf0TIA2RbPOj-8g (accessed April 22, 2019)

Statista. 2018. https://www.statista.com/statistics/265759/world-population-by-age-and-region/ (accessed April 22, 2019).

SucceedFeed.com/Howard Schultz Quotes. 2019. https://succeedfeed.com/howard-schultz-quotes/ (accessed April 22, 2019).

Talisker Whisky Challenge. 2019. https://taliskerwhiskyatlanticchallenge.com/ (accessed April 21, 2019).

Teigan, C. 2019. On Twitter @ChrissyTeigan. https://twitter.com/chrissyteigen (accessed April 22, 2019).

The Book Fairies. https://ibelieveinbookfairies.com/about-the-book-fairies/ (accessed April 22, 2019).

The Economist Group. 2019. https://economistgroup.com/ (accessed April 22, 2019).

The Global Media Monitoring Project Report. 2015. http://whomakesthenews.org/gmmp (accessed April 22, 2019).

The Guardian. 2002. https://theguardian.com/politics/2000/jun/08/uk.labour3

Time. May 27, 2011. http://techland.time.com/2011/05/27/study-53-of-youngsters-would-choose-technology-over-sense-of-smell/ (accessed April 22, 2019).

Times Education Supplement. Afghanistan Literacy Appeal. 2002. https://tes.com/news/how-you-can-raise-funds-0 (accessed April 21, 2019).

Times of India. 2015. https://economictimes.indiatimes.com/cultural-instincts-of-different-societies-have-major-implications-for-indian-mncs/articleshow/48186271.cms (accessed April 22, 2019).

todayshow.com. 2019. BP CEO Tom Hayward. https://youtube.com/watch?v=MTdKa9eWNFw (accessed April 22, 2019).

TopHashTags.com. 2019. www.top-hashtags.com (accessed April 22, 2019).

Tour de France. 2019. https://letour.fr/en/landing-page (accessed April 22, 2019).

Turnstyles Football Academy. 2019. https://loveturnstyles.co.uk/ (accessed April 22, 2019).

Twitter. 2019. https://twitter.com/ (accessed April 22, 2019).

UNESCO. 2013. http://unesco.org/new/en/unesco/events/prizes-and-celebrations/celebrations/international-days/world-radio-day-2013/statistics-on-youth/ (accessed April 22, 2019).

United Nations. 2013. https://news.un.org/en/story/2013/03/435102-deputy-un-chief-calls-urgent-action-tackle-global-sanitation-crisis (accessed April 22, 2019).

United Nations. 2019. https://un.org/en/ (accessed April 22, 2019).

Unwrpd. 2019. https://unwrpd.com/about (accessed April 22, 2019).

Vastu, S.G. 2019. https://vastushastraguru.com/ (accessed April 22, 2019).

Vij, V. 2019. On Instagram. @theurbanlog (accessed April 22, 2019).

Vivida Productions. 2019. https://vivida.co.uk/ (accessed April 22, 2019).

Williamson, M. 2019. https://marianne.com/ (accessed April 22, 2019).

Wilson, A.J. 2019. On LinkedIn. https://linkedin.com/in/drjonwilson/?originalSubdomain=uk (accessed April 22, 2019).

Women Economic Forum. 2019. https://wef.org.in/ (accessed April 22, 2019).

Yandex. 2019. https://yandex.com/ (accessed April 22, 2019).

Yousafzai, M. 2019. On Twitter. @Malala (accessed April 21, 2019).

YouTube Press. 2019. https://youtube.com/intl/en-GB/yt/about/press/ (accessed April 22, 2019).

YouTube. 2019. www.youtube.com (accessed April 22, 2019).

Zappos. 2019. https://zappos.com/ (accessed April 22, 2019).

About the Author

Sangeeta Waldron is a multi-award-winning public relations (PR) and media professional with over two decades' worth of publicity, branding, communications, crisis management, media, and social media experience. She started out her career writing speeches for a previous UK prime minister and cabinet ministers, and has also worked at the top level for big, powerful global brands, which includes global communications director for the Economist Group; working for The Times Education Supplement; the Mayor of London; World Health Organization; Cass Business School; and charities such as Breast Cancer Campaign.

Today, she runs her own successful London-based PR agency, Serendipity PR & Media Ltd, working across business, arts, culture, and books in growth international markets. She is also an award-winning journalist, specializing in sustainability and corporate social responsibility, where her stories have been picked up by the United Nations and *The Guardian* newspaper.

An international speaker, she also sits on different boards and believes in the power of paying it forward.

Twitter: @SangeetaWaldron and you can find me on LinkedIn under the same name.

Index

OTHER TITLES IN OUR PUBLIC RELATIONS COLLECTION

Don W. Stacks and Donald K. Wright, Editors

- *Excellence in Internal Communication Management* by Rita Linjuan Men and Shannon A. Bowen
- *A Professional and Practitioner's Guide to Public Relations Research, Measurement, and Evaluation, Third Edition* by David Michaelson and Donald W. Stacks
- *A Communication Guide for Investor Relations in an Age of Activism* by Marcia W. DiStaso, David Michaelson, and John Gilfeather
- *Corporate Communication Crisis Leadership: Advocacy and Ethics* by Ronald C. Arnett, Sarah M. Deluliis, and Matthew Corr
- *Public Relations Ethics: Senior PR Pros Tell Us How to Speak Up and Keep Your Job* by Marlene S. Neill and Amy Oliver Barnes
- *The New Era of the CCO: The Essential Role of Communication in a Volatile World* by Roger Bolton, Don W. Stacks, and Eliot Mizrachi

Announcing the Business Expert Press Digital Library

Concise e-books business students need for classroom and research

This book can also be purchased in an e-book collection by your library as

- a one-time purchase,
- that is owned forever,
- allows for simultaneous readers,
- has no restrictions on printing, and
- can be downloaded as PDFs from within the library community.

Our digital library collections are a great solution to beat the rising cost of textbooks. E-books can be loaded into their course management systems or onto students' e-book readers.
The **Business Expert Press** digital libraries are very affordable, with no obligation to buy in future years. For more information, please visit **www.businessexpertpress.com/librarians**. To set up a trial in the United States, please email **sales@businessexpertpress.com**.